REKINDLING
THE MAINLINE

New Life through New Churches

Stephen C. Compton

Foreword by Jackson W. Carroll

The Alban Institute

Scripture quotations, unless otherwise noted, are from the New Revised Standard Version of the Bible, copyright © 1989, Division of Christian Education of the National Council of Churches in the United States of America, and are used by permission.

Scripture quotations marked "KJV" are from The Holy Bible, King James Version.

Library of Congress Card Number 2002116300
ISBN 1-56699-279-6

07   06   05   04   03   VG   1   2   3   4   5   6   7   8   9   10

To Charlie and Zonie

Contents

Foreword

IN 1972, WHEN DEAN KELLEY DROPPED his bombshell of a book, *Why Conservative Churches Are Growing* (which he had initially titled *Why Liberal Churches Are Declining*), mainline Protestants suddenly realized that they had a serious problem: They were experiencing substantial membership decline, and at a time when conservative churches were growing rapidly. The mainline's losses were real, having begun in the early 1960s, and Kelley's book not only provided hard evidence of patterns of growth and decline; it also provoked much handwringing among mainline leaders. Many authors and church leaders attempted to explain the trends. Kelley's own theory was based on the mainline churches' lack of strictness in beliefs, in comparison to the staunch beliefs of conservative churches.

Other observers offered another popular explanation for mainline decline. They blamed mainline Protestant leaders—especially denominational officials and activist clergy—for their pursuit of a social-action agenda during the 1960s. First the civil rights movement came to the fore, and then the anti–Vietnam War effort. Clergy activism, so the explanation went, led to the defection of many disenchanted laity who did not share the clergy's social passion. This conflict reflected, as one interpreter described it, "a gathering storm in the churches."

As with all attempts to attribute the declines to a single cause, this explanation was unduly simplistic. Although significant lay-clergy conflict arose over denominational social activism, this discord was not the major cause of mainline declines, if indeed it was much of a factor at all.

In retrospect, we can see another connection between the social-action agenda of the mainline and declining membership that had a more important impact. In response to the civil rights movement and the general social ferment of the 1960s, mainline Protestants shifted their denominational outreach funding priorities away from starting new congregations in America's growing suburbs—an effort that had been a 1950s preoccupation. Instead, they provided funding for various social-justice ministries, especially in connection with civil rights. It was a laudable effort on the denominations' part to be faithful to the gospel in a turbulent time. But it had an important unintended effect on membership numbers. Throughout the '50s, new church starts had accounted for the majority of the membership growth within mainline denominations. When support for new-church development was cut, the number of new-church starts declined sharply, and so did membership. For example, the United Presbyterian Church (a predecessor denomination of the Presbyterian Church [U.S.A.]) had started an average of 70.1 new churches per year from 1950 to 1962. Between 1963 and 1973, however, the denomination established only 29.8 congregations per year, many of them intended primarily for ethnic-minority congregations. In contrast, the Southern Baptist Convention, which experienced no decline in membership during this period, started an average of 95.2 new congregations between 1963 and 1973. Indeed, many older mainline and conservative congregations, with aging constituents and locations away from population growth centers, had already been losing members throughout the 1950s, even as their denominations were growing rapidly as a result of the new suburban congregations. It was this shift in priorities, I believe, more than lay anger over church social action, that played a significant role in membership declines. Although this factor was not the only cause of mainline losses, it was an important one.

The lesson to be drawn from this source of membership loss is the one that Stephen Compton so ably demonstrates in this book: New-church development, including the creation of new congregations out of older ones, continues to be a key to denominational renewal and vitality. Given his broad and extensive experience with congregational development, Compton is supremely able to teach us about such renewal. The renewal he writes about, however, is not just in membership growth. Rather, it is a renewal of both spirit and practice that new congregations and transformed older ones bring to the larger church. As they introduce and carry out new ideas and practices, these new and renewed congregations perform, as Compton notes, an important research and development task for the church.

Although new congregations are often innovative, Compton does not praise innovation for the sake of innovation. Rather, new practices must be adopted in service of the gospel, connecting participants with the church's traditions even as they make the gospel accessible in a changing social context. The new congregations toward whose creation he works are distinctive communities of faith whose appeal is not novelty but authenticity.

Renewing a denomination that is top-heavy with older congregations is, nonetheless, more easily said than done. Not only are older congregations often located in contexts that make growth difficult; they often follow well-worn paths of church practice that are highly resistant to change. "But we have always done it this way!"—these are the seven last words of atrophied congregations. In regard to such resistance, Compton reports strategies that he has used to help many such congregations re-envision their ministries. He speaks, therefore, with the authority of long experience and provides important practical guidance about starting new congregations and renewing older ones. He also offers a valuable perspective on the kind of leadership—clergy and lay—needed for these tasks, including important words of advice for seminaries and programs of continuing theological education that train such leaders.

Drawing on analogies from jazz, pottery-making, and science, and on insights from chaos theory, the author encourages congregational leaders to improvise in ways appropriate to their context, while maintaining the main "melody" or message that the gospel provides. When such an approach is taken, conflict sometimes seems likely to create chaos, especially in efforts to renew older congregations. Yet rather than avoid it, congregations can embrace such dissension as an important catalyst for positive change.

Just as single-factor explanations do not account for all mainline membership decline, new-church development may not by itself be the only road to mainline renewal. But it is a crucial one, as the author makes abundantly and persuasively clear in this important book. I learned much from it, and I commend it with great enthusiasm.

Jackson W. Carroll

Preface

My FATHER, WHOSE PARENTS RAISED TOBACCO and reared seven kids, was brought up in a home where religious allegiance was shared between two very different traditions. My paternal grandfather considered himself a Primitive Baptist but was not a church member because he never felt himself *worthy,* a characteristic theological tenet of this strictly Calvinist sect. My grandmother, of Scots decent, was a member of the Presbyterian Church. Farm and family chores sometimes prevented church attendance, but mostly on Sundays she and her troupe of children trekked a few miles to Eno Presbyterian Church. My mother's family was Primitive Baptist through and through, and church was an every-Sunday event—men seated separately from women and children, no Sunday school, and a cappella singing.

My mother and father married in 1948, and I was born an early baby boomer in 1950. In their early years of marriage, my parents were what might today be called an "unchurched" couple. In 1953 a new church, Trinity Methodist, was organized on a site less than a mile from our home. This church was one of the first begun by the North Carolina Conference of the Methodist Church to reach a goal of establishing 70 churches in 70 months—an ambitious aim proposed by then Bishop Paul Neff Garber. Invited to become charter members of this fledgling congregation, we were welcomed into a community of faith that would forever change our family's history.

Led on a Pilgrimage

I am sure that without the nurturing of this church as I struggled to find answers to challenging faith questions, and as I discerned my call to the ordained ministry, I would not be writing this book. I will forever be grateful to my first pastors, Robert L. Nicks, Norwood L.

Jones, and Gayle T. Alexander; to numerous Sunday school and vacation Bible school teachers (in a way, their grape Kool-Aid and Oreo cookies were my first communion); and, most important, to my parents, Charlie and Zonie, whose lives epitomize what it means to be a Christian.

From the beginning of my faith journey as a new church member, I was led by God on a pilgrimage that once included leading a new church as its pastor, and that now includes the role I play guiding the North Carolina Conference of the United Methodist Church in planting, on average, five new churches each year.[1]

Rekindling Mainline Fires

I have become convinced that our grand old mainline denominations can have their spiritual passions rekindled as soon as we reclaim our past practice of planting new churches in large numbers, in every place where the gospel needs to be proclaimed. Unlike a short-term appended program for growth, new-church development has to become an ongoing component of the ministry and activity of mainline denominations.

In this book I argue for making new-church development the permanent, primary strategy for extending the reach of God's church into the hearts of people who do not yet know the joy and wholeness of life that comes from a relationship with God. This goal presents a considerable challenge to the prevailing mind-set of mainline denominations. To embrace it requires that we reconsider and clarify our denominational core values, beliefs, and practices. It means that nothing we have become can escape review, including our organizational structures, programs, staffing, funding, and decision-making processes. It means that ineffective activities will have to be let go; tired traditions will have to be refreshed; and opportunities will have to be given for new forms of church to dawn.

Perhaps I am naïve to think that this goal can be achieved. I recognize how difficult it could be to return matured mainline denominations to the pioneering, entrepreneurial, spirited attitude of a movement. Yet grand spiritual movements have come before, sweeping away the detritus of our human failings, making room for God's kingdom to rush in. This experience can happen, I believe, to the mainline church. In fact, some evidence suggests that the movement has begun already. Throughout many mainline denominations, pioneering laity, clergy, and local judicatory leaders are leading the way in new-church development, mostly without much direction or assistance from national judicatory offices. Goals are being set; money is being raised; leadership is being identified and trained; and sites are being selected. Considering the losses in membership and influence realized by the mainline in recent decades, it may sound overoptimistic to say that I think today is an exciting time to be part of the mainline church in America; clear signs are evident that these denominational sleeping giants are awakening to new life.

At a Fork in the Road

To help make the case for new-church development, I have included anecdotes to illustrate key points. Most are drawn directly from my experience as a church member and leader; some are generously lent to me by others; and some are fictionalized accounts based on my knowledge of actual events, communities, churches, and people.

The mainline church is on a great journey. The road it has followed has been a good one, well traveled. But today, the mainline stands at a fork in the road. One way, the wide path, is well-worn and familiar, and may lead to the mainline's demise. The other way, the narrow path, is mostly uncharted. It promises to lead travelers to new adventures as the church seeks to find its way in a 21st-century world. Which path the mainline chooses will determine whether it will become a better version of the late 20th-century church, or a new church whose mission is rekindled by God for a new day. I believe the narrow, less predictable route is the mainline's best choice, and I believe that new congregations will lead us in this venturesome journey.

Acknowledgments

I OWE MUCH TO A GREAT MANY PEOPLE for making it possible for me to write this book. It has been written during a difficult period in my life. Without the encouragement and support of many friends and family members, the manuscript would not exist. I learned in the past year the true value of long-cultivated friendships.

I am especially thankful for the assistance I have received from Camille Yorkey, new-church planter par excellence. Her responses to my interview questions found in chapter 6 reveal only a bit of the grand wisdom she has regarding new-church leadership. The mainline needs thousands like her.

Two bishops, C. P. Minnick, Jr., and Marion M. Edwards, have played instrumental roles in pushing United Methodism's North Carolina Conference to the forefront of new-church development ministry. They have given me the opportunity to fly in the wind of this emerging movement, and for that I am extraordinarily appreciative.

My administrative assistant, Nancy Koontz, has endured me and encouraged me as I have tried to juggle book-writing and my "real" work for the conference's office of congregational development. Thank you for your patience, Nancy, and for just being there one more time when I needed something done ASAP.

I would be negligent were I not to thank the real champions of new-church development—the pastors who risk so much to be pioneers in this challenging ministry of church extension. Without knowing it (or perhaps they do!), they have been my lab rats in an important research experiment. They have run the maze well, and they continue to teach the church and me much about how new communities of faith, fertile with vital ministry, are created. To my best friend, Bill Presnell, I wish to say that if I ever grow up to be a real preacher,

I hope I will be just like you. You are an inspiration to me and to many others, and the richness of your leadership shapes much of what I have to say in this book.

I am deeply indebted to my editors, Beth Ann Gaede and Jean Caffey Lyles. Early in this project's development, Beth stated that her job was to make me look good. I dared not tell her how great the challenge would be to accomplish her goal. Her critical eye and generous suggestions for improvement of this book have been the key to any success that this book may achieve. Jean's advice and assistance have been equally valuable to me. With her witty remarks and ultrasharp pencil, she has shown me how to put my sometimes befuddled ideas into comprehensible English. Jean's magic touch is evident in every chapter of this book.

I must say a special word about my two sons, Matthew and Clay. They have endured my rantings about crazy church people; they have moved with me from parsonage to parsonage without complaint; they have worn the mantle of "preacher's kid" well, and they have forgiven me for my many absences when the demands of church leadership took me away too many nights and weekends. But, most important, they have loved me, and for this love, I will always be a better person. My greatest pleasure is derived from being called their dad.

My parents are my best advocates, and their love for me is bigger than I deserve. I dedicate this book to them. If any good comes from this book, its value is due to all they have done to make the church an important part of my life.

Chapter One

Who's Killing
My Old Church?

*Change is avalanching upon our heads and most people
are grotesquely unprepared to cope with it.*

—Alvin Toffler

*[God] has made everything suitable for its time; more-
over he has put a sense of past and future into their
minds.*

—Ecclesiastes 3:11a-b

We've never done it that way before.

—Anonymous church leader

STEP BACK IN TIME WITH ME. It's 4 P.M. on Sunday, December 20, 1958,
in McDade's Crossroads, a bucolic southeastern U.S. community
whose landscape is dotted with silos, log barns, and clapboard-sided
farmhouses. McDade's (that's the way residents of this rural community refer to it) was settled by Scots Presbyterians late in the 18th
century. Mostly they were tobacco farmers, tilling small to medium-
sized plots ranging from a hundred to several hundred acres. Before
the Civil War, slaves had been held and worked by some community
families, but mostly crops were raised and harvested by all members
of large families whose households varied from eight to eighteen
people. After 1865, some of the former slaves stayed on as sharecroppers. Occasionally, white workers also signed on as sharecroppers. A
sharecropper worked without wage, depending for a living on a small

1

percentage of the proceeds from the sale of the tobacco crop at the
end of the season. A few were given a plot of an acre or so to raise
tobacco on their own, space for a garden, and perhaps enough room
to graze a milk cow.

Modest but sound frame houses accommodate McDade's residents.
Laborers live on the farms in smallish cottages consisting of a room
or two. Hedgerows separate yards from fields. On most farms the
mule barn exceeds the family farmhouse in size. On a successful farm,
mules are second in importance only to the labor of the family's children and the other laborers. Chopping (a term used to describe the
incessant process of hoeing weeds from around the plants), pulling
"suckers," topping the blooms from plants, tying and hanging tobacco in barns to cure—these are tasks ably accomplished by human
labor. But breaking new ground, plowing planted rows of the crop,
and pulling heavy-laden sleds of tobacco from field to barn are tasks
left to the strong backs of the family's sometimes stubborn but beloved mules.

A Church of Big Families

In McDade's, you can always predict where the community residents
will gather on the Sunday before Christmas. All of the community's
families gather at Elgin Memorial Presbyterian Church to watch as
Mary, Joseph, the baby Jesus, angels, shepherds, and wise men come
to fill the chancel—with most of the players dressed in bathrobes and
bedecked with cotton-ball beards.

This year, the part of baby Jesus is played by the youngest member of the MacGregor family. Little Sam, as he is called, is the 10th
grandchild of Ralph and Carrie MacGregor, whose eight children are
bringing great joy to the couple by increasing the MacGregor household. The MacGregors were among the earliest settlers in the community. Ralph, his father before him, and his grandfather before that,
have all been looked to as leaders in the church. In fact, for generations no major decision regarding the church has been made without
the tacit approval of the MacGregor clan, and no one seems to mind
that this is the case. The MacGregors are good people, and they seem
always to have the best interests of the church and community at
heart.

The parts of Mary and Joseph are played by siblings, Alice and Charlie Kerr. Joseph's robe, a bit tattered around hem and collar, has been worn by three generations of Kerrs in numerous Christmas pageants. This very robe has served the Kerr children before—once as a shepherd, and three times as a wise man. This year the roles of angels, shepherds, and wise men, along with variously costumed barnyard animals with noticeably anthropomorphic features, are filled by brothers, sisters, cousins, and neighbors representing the MacGregors, Kerrs, McDades, and of course the Elgins, whose family gained naming rights when the church was formed in 1832 by giving an acre of land for the cause of erecting a Presbyterian house of worship.

Props for the production are managed by the four McDade boys, ranging in age from 13 to 16; costumes and makeup are administered by teenage cousins Mary, Susan, Elizabeth, and Marnie Kerr. At the piano is Miss Julia Elgin, matriarch of the Elgin bloodline, and longtime piano teacher at the nearby community school. She has never married, but after the influenza-related deaths of both her mother and father, she successfully managed the family farm and reared six younger siblings. For as long as anyone can remember, she has always been called simply "Miss Julia."

The Rev. Henry J. Mitchell, a small man, but one possessing great presence in the pulpit when preaching the word of God, serves as narrator. This fine man's home visits are always well received by the families of the community. Though the church's preachers are always well-loved and respected as spiritual leaders, members learned long ago not to become too attached to one, since few stay at Elgin Memorial much more than two or three years before moving on to new calls elsewhere.

On this cold winter afternoon, the pews are filled with kin and neighbors from at least 10 nearby farms. No one is a stranger. Filling nearly two rows on both right and left sides of the center aisle are members of the MacGregor family. There is Sam, father of Little Sam (the baby Jesus), his wife, Sally, and their three older sons and two daughters. Increasingly, Sam is responsible for operating the family farm, and everyone expects that he will continue to farm it, as his father and two grandfathers before him did. Already, Sam hopes that at least one of his children will take up the farm after him. Most people in the church expect that Big Sam will take over the role of his father as chief leader of the church. Ralph's memory is not what it used to be, and his arthritis makes it harder every year for him to look after the church building and grounds and the cemetery. That's just the way it has been in McDade's Crossroads for as long as anyone can remember. As one generation ages and passes on, the next generation steps up to continue the traditions of family, community, and church. As long as this has been the case, Elgin Memorial has held its own in membership, attendance, and ability to meet its financial obligations.

From Generation to Generation

This fictionalized, and somewhat idealized, snapshot of a once-typical American scene demonstrates how the majority of American churches were shaped and perpetuated—not so much by outreach programs or overt evangelistic effort, but by large families whose progeny held membership and leadership for generations. These mostly rural community churches were formed when the country was largely agrarian, during what futurist Alvin Toffler calls the agricultural, or first wave of sociocultural and community development, primarily in the 19th century.[1] One writer describes the time this way:

> The nineteenth century was the heyday of American Protestant expansion, driven largely by the perceived need to bring those who were settling the frontier into the Protestant fold. From this perspective revivalism, voluntary associations, camp meetings, and the circuit rider can be seen as parts of a greater whole—attempts to respond to the realities presented by the increasingly rural nature of American settlement."[2]

Exodus of the Young

Many features of 19th-century rural America changed in the 20th century. My grandfather was a sixth-generation representative of family farming in the southeastern United States. I suspect that he expected that at least one of his children would carry on the family tradition of farming. But when the United States entered World War II, his sons went off to Europe to serve the nation in the Allies' fight to stop Hitler and his Nazi forces. Not only did this experience change their worldview; in addition, the GI Bill made it possible for them to leave

home, family, and farm; to get an education, and to pursue an altogether different life. In fact, I have heard my father say that when he
joined the Army, he vowed to himself that, should he survive the war
and return home, he would never farm tobacco again. True to his
word, he married a city girl, took a business-school course, became a
bookkeeper, and built an attractive little house next to his brother's
in a new suburb. Today not one of the children lives on or farms the
rural homestead.

In the North Carolina Conference of the United Methodist
Church, an area composed of the state's 56 easternmost counties,
most of its more than 840 extant constituent churches were formed
during Toffler's defined first-wave era of American settlement. In fact,
741 Methodist churches were established in the area in the 19th
century.[3]

The founding of Chestnut Ridge United Methodist Church is typical of the period. James Cheek, an early Chestnut Ridge participant,
recollects its history as a camp-meeting ground:

> In my early boyhood they still had camp meetings there. A row of log
> cabins was built fifty to one hundred yards from the church. In these
> cabins, some of the families would stay through the meeting, one
> member going back and forth to take care of the stock at home.
>
> Not far from the church, there was an arbor under which they
> held meeting when the weather was suitable. It had a high pulpit,
> mourner's bench and straw all around in front of the pulpit.
>
> I can see those old circuit riders mounted on their horses, with
> their saddlebags. They would ride up to a tree, dismount and hitch
> their horse to a swinging limb and walk slowly and reverently through
> the grounds shaking hands with the brethren.[4]

This bygone era of rural church establishment, when the majority
of Protestant churches and church members resided in such settings,
is unlikely to be repeated. The migration of people from rural to
metropolitan locales escalated in the latter half of the 20th century.
According to the Bureau of the Census, the population of the United
States located in nonmetropolitan areas has shifted dramatically from
43.9 percent of the total in 1950 to 19.9 percent in 1998. Most of
this movement has been from rural areas to suburban neighborhoods,
with 23.3 percent living in suburbs in 1950, increasing to 49.9 percent

in 1998. Central city population totals changed by less than 3 percent during the same period.[5]

What effect has all of this change in rural America had on mainline Protestant churches? The answer to this question begins to explain who or what is to blame for the significant declines in once-mighty mainline denominations like the Presbyterians, Lutherans, and Methodists.

The health of old mainline denominations was for many decades reliant upon the health of their mostly small rural and often kinship-constituted congregations. The well-being of these churches was ensured by the predictable replacement of one generation of members and leaders by their children and grandchildren. The *alpha leader*, my term for the primary influencer of the congregation, could relinquish most, if not all, of the role to a child from the next generation in time to mentor and guide this new alpha leader into a top position. Then, in the next generation, another leader was handed the mantle of leadership in the same way.

Membership in these churches was multigenerational, with as many as five generations of a single family represented. Disruption in the pattern of family perpetuation of membership has led to critical changes in these once extraordinarily stable congregations. Availability of reliable means of contraception contributed to a reduction in family size. With the exodus of young generations from these rural communities to pursue higher education and nonagricultural jobs, the alpha leaders have had no one within the family to whom the leadership mantle could be passed. In many cases, aging influencers have tried to extend and maintain their gatekeeping role to preserve the church and its place in the community. Without new, younger generations of members (traditionally the children, grandchildren, and great-grandchildren of the church's primary families) to replace the oldest generation, however, these once multigenerational churches have become almost monogenerational, with a higher and higher average age of membership.

Rise and Demise of the Village Church

The loss of membership from rural churches in the late 19th and early 20th centuries was somewhat attenuated by the mainline denominations' establishment of new churches in new villages, towns, and cities, in what Toffler defines as the industrial, or second wave of sociocultural and community development.[6] In *Rural Ministry: The Shape of the Renewal to Come*, Shannon Jung, et al., state that Toffler's second wave

> focuses on the expansion of cities at the expense of the countryside in land, people, influence and power. The way of the factory became the organizing principle of everyday life. When the cities began to grow because of industrialization, a common model was to build a factory and cluster around it housing for the workers and for management. The concept was an adaptation of the English mill village. . . . Generally, for the first two generations of this era, the village church model simply was moved to the city. The urban mill villages had a chapel or two for the workers. It duplicated many of the practices of the rural village church. The primary difference was that the seasons and rhythms of the industry replaced the seasons of the soil at the center of the life of the congregation. This sameness was appropriate because the new urbanites were mostly ex-ruralites.[7]

Ca-Vel Church is a good example of a mill-village chapel. Founded and funded by textile-mill owners, this small-membership church served the mill workers and their families for several generations. Its history is much like that of thousands of similar chapels:

> Entire families frequently worked in the same mill. Often, the families, having few resources of their own, lived in low-rent, mill-owned houses, shopped at the mill-owned store, worshiped in mill-supported churches, and when there was time, learned in mill-operated schools. This was the core of the mill village phenomenon.[8]

The Rise of Urbanization

For the most part, this pattern of urbanization and industrialization persisted through the first half of the 20th century. Originally country folk, my mother's family members did mill work in Virginia, then followed jobs to the mill villages of Altamahaw and Ossipee in North Carolina, and eventually to the city of Burlington, for which the former textile giant, Burlington Industries, is named.

In the first half of the 20th century, at the height of the shift of people from rural to industrial jobs and communities, Methodism's

North Carolina Conference began 319 churches, many of these in textile mill communities like Burlington, Haw River, Roanoke Rapids (where some say striking J.P. Stevens workers gave rise to the story of movie heroine Norma Rae), and Erwin (once the self-proclaimed world denim capital).

The mill village provided a ready supply of potential members for the village church. In many cases, families continued to be as large as typical rural families, with multiple generations represented in a single household. Some mill owners would supply housing only to families that could provide at least three workers.[9] Women and children made up a significant portion of the workforce in textile mills, and working conditions were abominable. Whether the work was in coal mines, glass factories, or cotton mills, many of these laborers "owed their souls to the company store."

Yet compared to the bare subsistence lifestyle and the uncertainties of farming on small plots of worn-out land, the relative security of factory work with a small cash wage, plus housing, a church, and occasionally a school, mill work had its attractions. Some formerly rural Americans still speak with pride about the first member of the family who left the farm to do "public work"—usually meaning a job in town that didn't involve hoeing, picking cotton, or feeding any creatures except the kids.

Numerous factors have led to the demise of the mill-village phenomenon of urban development. Take your pick: the boll weevil; increased mechanization; consolidation of small, local mill operations into large industrial conglomerates; and more. But as in rural farming communities, World War II may have had the most profound effect on these industrial communities.

Like the many young adults from farm families who as veterans took advantage of the GI Bill to get a free education and training in a nonagricultural field, many children of mill workers followed the same pattern. The added benefit of low-interest mortgage loans allowed many a veteran to become the first in the family to own a home. The war had drawn many more women into the workforce, and many chose to remain employed after the war's end. Typically, postwar couples had smaller families than their parents and grandparents had had. The mills were left with a smaller pool of available workers, and the village churches had fewer young members and fewer adherents overall to carry the mantle of leadership into succeeding generations.

In the mill village, as in the rural community, once the pattern of family perpetuation of membership was broken, it took only one or two generations (about 40 years)—if no other source of growth was found and accommodated—for the church to reach a crisis point, leaving its effectiveness as a community of faith and its very survival in question. This trend has been evident in both rural and old industrial communities since at least 1950 and, to some extent, since the late 19th and the early 20th century. Is it any wonder, with so many of the mainline congregations having been started in these two kinds of settings, that so many are in distress or have already met their demise?

Effects of Neighborhood Transition

Baraca Church, located on the corner of Redgate and Clark streets, was established in the first decade of the 20th century in the city of Rocky Mount, North Carolina. This small southern city straddles the line separating Nash and Edgecombe counties. The county line is clearly demarcated by railroad tracks running not only along that line, but also directly through the center of the downtown business district. Not long after its founding, the church name was changed to "Clark Street," clearly indicating its station as a neighborhood church. The church was located on the blue-collar Edgecombe County side of the tracks, a fact unambiguously known by all who lived in the vicinity. Rocky Mount has produced a regional bank of some prominence, and it is the birthplace of the nationally known Hardee's fast-food chain. But all of the most prominent businesses, neighborhoods, and "First churches" in town have been located on the Nash County side of the line. Clark Street's location was clearly the place where reliable, working-class families chose to live. Most of the community's residents were railroad workers. This was the site of a roundhouse and shops for the Atlantic Coast Line and later, the Seaboard Coastline railroad. Other residents and church members were mail carriers, teachers, and retail sales clerks in nearby shops. The community was dotted with locally owned grocery stores and full-service gas stations. The streets were lined with neat clapboard bungalows exhibiting tiny but neatly trimmed lawns. A neighborhood school was merely blocks from most residences. It was an all-white neighborhood, whose demographic origins didn't have to be explained, and that never elicited apologies in early 20th-century southern venues like Rocky Mount.

From its beginning, the church served its community well. Its membership, numbering nearly 400 in the early 1980s, was loyal to its task and excelled at looking after its own parish family. At least two ministers were raised up from its ranks. The congregation ran a sizable and spirited youth ministry in the 1960s.

By the early 1980s, change began to envelop the Clark Street community as the railroad, once an economic mainstay of the area, closed its operations. Locally owned and operated mom-and-pop businesses lost their market to larger stores like the A&P grocery chain. In the 1970s the community's young adults, among the first wave of the nation's maturing baby boomers, had failed to return from professional schools or colleges to work in the community, and the average age of the neighborhood's residents rose speedily. For many working-class American families in the 1960s, '70s, and '80s, their children were the first in the lineage to obtain college degrees.

The effects of community change were clearly reflected in the membership of Clark Street Church. In less than two decades the congregation fell from its apex of activity to a church characterized by low attendance, little programming, nearly nonexistent children's and youth ministries, and financial instability. To sustain its ministry, the church was "yoked" with another small-membership church nearly 10 miles away. They shared a pastor, but did little to interact otherwise.

As more and more residents of the community moved away and others died, homes were bought up in large numbers by absentee owners, who in turn rented the houses to "outsiders." For the most part, the new residents of the Clark Street neighborhood were low-income African Americans. By the early 1990s, the majority population in the once all-white community was African American. Drugs and crime followed poverty into the community. The local school was closed and ceded to local vandals.

If any effort was made to welcome and incorporate the community's new neighbors into the life of Clark Street Church, it was unsuccessful. In 1994, the church was discontinued at a time when its average weekly worship attendance had declined to fewer than 15 worshipers. Ironically, its neighborhood population was growing, and the average age of the nearby households was much younger than that of the church's remaining members. The need for ministry and service in the vicinity had never been greater.[10]

Affecting not only small-town communities like Rocky Mount, neighborhood transition has had considerable effect on churches in major urban locations.

Endowed, Resplendent—Empty

A large northeastern U.S. city, the state's capital, is the site of one of the nation's outstanding church edifices. Erected in the 1920s, the neo-Gothic structure boasts high-quality craftsmanship in its hand-hewn stone facade and high-art stained-glass windows. Inside, its voluminous nave allows seating for 500. Its organ prominently displays many ranks of pipes that reverberate regularly with the sounds of Bach, Vivaldi, and Buxtehude. The choirmaster prides himself on the fact that his choir sings music that, in his words, is "strong," requiring hard work for the choir to learn. A side chapel is resplendent with the same level of workmanship displayed in the sanctuary. Classrooms are numerous and spacious. The structure and its rich furnishings are immaculately maintained. Upon viewing this grand church building, one need not ask to know that at the time of its construction, some of the city's most prominent, influential, and affluent members were among its flock. For some time, the church has been host to a large meals program and thrift shop for the city's homeless and impoverished residents, a day-care center operated for children of low-income families, and a Spanish-speaking congregation. From an outsider's viewpoint, this congregation's pulpit would seem a prestigious appointment for any minister called to its leadership. But looks can be deceiving.

In fact, fewer than 100 people gather there for worship each week. Eighty-five people have been members of the church for more than 50 years. In large part, the facility is maintained and the senior pastor's ample salary (the highest in the denomination's region) is paid by a generous endowment, to which more than $1 million has been added in recent years. One-third of the church's annual income is realized from endowment earnings. The meal ministry, thrift shop, and day care are sponsored not by the church, but by outside community agencies that pay rent to the congregation for use of the space. One-third of the church's annual budget is raised from rents from these nonprofit community groups. The Hispanic congregation described above was not part of the church's ministry and was asked to find another meeting location. Church workers did not like having "outsiders" use their facilities.

The church's neighborhood is not unlike many aging urban landscapes today. Townhouses and commercial buildings, once well kept, are now deteriorated tenements. Trash and discarded wine bottles and drug paraphernalia, including needles and glittering, broken glass syringes, litter walkways, alleys, and curbs. On some blocks, boarded windows and doors appear to outnumber those showing exposed, unbroken panes of glass. On nearly every block one or more storefront churches are flourishing, some boasting spirited Pentecostal-style worship with upbeat music, emotional outbursts by ecstatic participants, and animated preaching. Others offer one-stop service for salvation, a hot meal, and drug counseling. This area of the city is racially and ethnically diverse. Little about this church's community is reflected in the congregation's makeup or in its own ministries. Like chocolate on rice, the church and its community don't go together. Evidently, on its present course, this church's demise is imminent and would have come sooner were it not for the endowment lifeboat keeping it afloat.

Waiting for the New Neighbors

In some instances, a church endures multiple community transitions. This is the case with Cokesbury Church, a small African American congregation located near an Interstate beltway looping through a metropolitan area with a population of roughly one million. In the early 1960s, the church began its life as an all-white suburban congregation. In the decades that followed, the surrounding community changed from a nearly all-white population to a neighborhood of mostly lower-income, African American residents. The church, though always a small-membership body, was successful in its transition to a mostly African American membership.

In recent years, the neighborhood has again begun to undergo demographic transition. Today its population is made up of a mixture of middle- and low-income African Americans, Hispanics, Asians, and whites. Despite its past successes in dealing with change in its neighborhood, today the church is on the brink of closure, having at best a couple of dozen aging members. A white female pastor was assigned to lead the church in an attempt to broaden its outreach, without success. The church is now led by an African American lay-woman who gives a few hours of service each week to the task—while holding down a full-time professional position, plus serving as the pastoral leader of another small church nearby.

Each of these stories illustrates how difficult it is for long-established churches to adapt to fundamental demographic shifts in their communities, so that their memberships and ministries reflect today's mission needs and not those of bygone eras. American people are increasingly mobile, often choosing to live in places where they have no connections to the community, its people, or its organizations. Immigration, especially of Latinos, is quickly changing the makeup and complexity of many American communities. Many public institutions and private businesses adapt to these changes, even if slowly and reluctantly. Police departments, schools, and hospitals employ bilingual workers; grocery chains add an international array of foods to their shelves to attract and serve new customers; newsstands and music outlets provide multiple-language editions of their offerings; bank ATMs offer to conduct financial transactions in a choice of languages; radio stations increasingly offer blocks of broadcast time to spinning Latino, Native American, and Reggae tunes. Yet, many congregations seem to think that they have already become the ideal church, and so they wait quietly and patiently for their new, and vastly different, neighbors to come around. "We're always here, and they're always welcome [to do it our way]" seems to be the unspoken but clearly conveyed motto of too many such churches. And yet we wonder, "Who's killing my old church?"

The Usefulness of Tradition

Religious researcher and former Marquette University faculty member Donald L. Metz writes:

> On the one hand, the congregation is in the business of maintaining a tradition with its peculiar symbols . . . On the other hand, the congregation may try to alter an aspect of the social environment in

the course of which effort it runs the risk of alienating some persons. Since the congregation depends upon these persons for its resources, it may have to compromise some of its goals in order to attain others."[11]

The dilemma faced by many churches today rests upon the fact that tradition (the way we've done it before) is both valuable and detrimental to the church. Jackson W. Carroll, professor emeritus of religion and society at Duke Divinity School, and director of the J. M. Ormond Center for Research, Development, and Planning, says, "[T]o ignore the churches' traditions is to ignore an important means of grace. The accumulated wisdom of the church's practices as it has struggled through the years with what it means to be faithful is a rich resource for inspiration and guidance as we face our own challenges. Our traditions re-present that wisdom and make it available to us."[12] On the other hand, being held hostage by tradition is an unconscionable denial of the transcendent nature of God.

A Church's Life Cycle

As a young, 53-year-old, middle-aged person (I intend to live to be 106), I am becoming increasingly (and sometimes agonizingly) aware of the natural life cycle of human beings. I remember when misery was a bee sting, not back pain; when fatigue was what my feet felt after a series of 10-mile days on the Appalachian trail, not breathlessness from climbing the stairs to my office. As biological beings, we are born; we mature and grow through adolescence; we become somewhat sedentary adults; we decline in old age; and we die. We all know the routine. A number of scholars have noticed how congregations often mimic the life cycle of biological organisms.[13]

Each year, I work as a consultant with dozens of churches, and through years of accumulated experience in ministry as a pastor and in congregational development, I have found the effects of this life cycle on congregations to be readily apparent. Demonstrating this life cycle and helping a church find itself in the progressive route between life and death has become an important tool for helping church leaders find their way out of stability and decline to vital ecclesial health.

Stage One: Birth

The birth stage of the life cycle is brief, almost momentary in the scale of time usually associated with the full life of a congregation. (It must be noted that in almost no other way is a particular scale of time important to an understanding of a church's life cycle. The duration of each stage is so variable from one church to the next that it is impossible to characterize each stage by assigning a stated length of time to it.) No period in the life of a church is more responsible than the birth stage, despite its brevity, for defining the congregation's mission and self-identity. No person is more responsible for shaping this first definition of the church than the founding pastor. In a lasting way, the character of the first pastor's leadership and role in shaping the values and practices of a fledgling congregation is imprinted on the church. First, or charter, members, a core group of supporters who join with the pastor in giving birth to the church, also contribute to defining its character. The process of founding a church, discerning its first mission, and putting in place the infrastructure necessary to make ministry happen, is often a life-transforming experience for the pastor and the first members. They do not give up easily on their first vision of the church, and their collective imprint is likely to remain on the church for a very long time. The values of the church are often set at this time. Saying you are a "charter member" carries value for those who were in the core group, and often this value is respected by many second-tier members.

Many benefits for effective ministry are associated with this potent defining period in the life of a church. Mostly, the church begins with a clean page, figuratively speaking, without prior traditions or practices dictating what will be done in and by this new church. Every new member has chosen to be part of the founding of the congregation; this experience is frequently a spiritually life-transforming event. The values of the congregation are freshly chosen, usually as the result of prayerful study of the community context, of scripture, and of the historic tenets of the church and its sponsoring denomination, if it has one. The unparalleled clarity in this stage about the church's values and purpose, goals and objectives, may rarely be so evident again. This clarity of purpose results in intentional outreach, growth, and effectiveness that generate interest in the church, attract new members, and create support from many sources. For this reason, it is not at all unusual for a new church, meeting in temporary

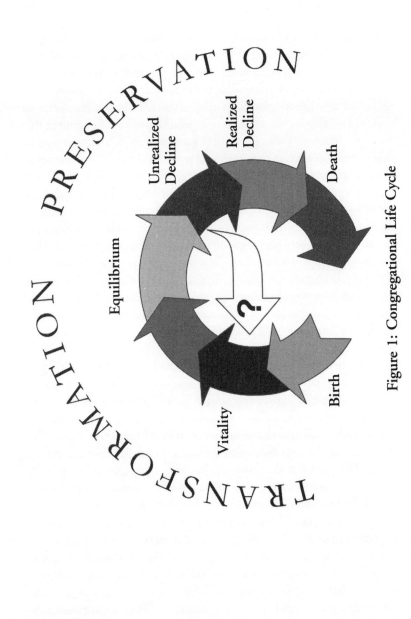

Figure 1: Congregational Life Cycle

quarters, with limited financial and leadership resources, to grow quickly to become two, five, or even 10 times larger in average worship attendance and membership than many nearby older churches serving in the same demographic setting.

Stage Two: Vitality

In the second, or vitality stage of the life cycle, the church often enjoys an extended period of growth—in membership, activity, and funding. This is a time for renovating or building additions to its church facilities, and for moving toward fulfillment of the congregation's stated mission. This vitality stage is usually built upon the foundation laid at the birth of the church, a footing rarely abandoned. The emerging congregation begins to shape and define its values. Is the church multicultural in makeup? Is worship offered in more than one language or more than one style? What is expected of members of this church? How are the traditional holy seasons observed and celebrated? In short, what traditions will we adopt that are compatible with our chosen values?

I was once assigned as a pastor to lead a newly created congregation that had been operating for 18 months before my arrival. The founding pastor had led the church to increase its average worship attendance to 80, with about 50 members. Personal concerns led the pastor to make an early exit from the congregation to pursue an advanced theological degree. Upon my arrival, about 20 of the adult charter members remained in place. One of these made a quick departure after my first Sunday at worship, charging that I had been sent by my bishop to change everything the members and their first pastor had set out to do. (That was not the case.)

The church had taken the name Saint Francis United Methodist. It is a bit unusual for a non-apostolic saint's name to be used by churches of the denomination. In addition, the pastor had decided— in consultation, I am sure, with the core group—that holy communion would be celebrated at every worship service. Although our Anglican founder, John Wesley, would no doubt be pleased with this practice, this too was extraordinary for United Methodist congregations at the time (and continues to be today). Communion was served by intinction—with worshipers dipping the wafer into the common cup rather than drinking from it. (Intinction is still such a "new" practice for many Methodists that when it is used, celebrants usually have to explain it before worshipers come to the table.) In another break with Methodist tradition, "real" wine was used (United Methodist folklore says that despite the concern for recovering, active, and potential alcoholics often cited to justify the use of grape juice in communion services, the truth is related to the fact that a certain Mr. Welch, a manufacturer of grape juice, was a staunch Methodist with no little degree of influence in the church.)

Notwithstanding my one skeptical, vocal core member's doubts and objections, I was cautious about changing the church's practices willy-nilly before trying to understand why such customs had been chosen to define its identity as a new church.

As it turned out, the name Saint Francis was selected by the core members while meeting in the "Upper Room," an upstairs garage office, to study the life of Saint Francis of Assisi on the 500th anniversary of his birth. The church was being formed in an affluent new community, and Francis's choice to deny his own legitimate claim to wealth, and to serve the poor, struck a chord with the founding members. As a result, the church became extraordinarily involved in outreach and service ministries in communities affected by poverty. Worshipers found that communion by intinction created a meaningful connection between those serving the bread and wine (the pastor and lay servers) and those coming close to the table to receive the elements. (Typically, American Methodists, in a very private posture, kneel at a rail in front of, or surrounding, the communion table, and receive individual cups of juice and a small portion of bread or a wafer.) As for the wine—historical precedents abound, but perhaps its use made the members of St. Francis feel less guilty about sipping wine at home!

Surprisingly, these somewhat unusual choices (for United Methodists in the 1980s) became valuable tools for attracting new members. The church began to attract significant numbers of young couples, one partner a Roman Catholic and the other a Protestant (often not Methodist). We became their "comfortable solution," bridging their formative faith experiences and bringing them into relationship with a church that seemed to honor many of the beliefs and practices important to them before their marriage.

I relished the practice of serving the communion elements by intinction. Wearing name tags was a requisite practice at Saint Francis. As each person came to the table, I could see the name tag, and I used the communicant's name when presenting the bread or wine. By then, the sermon was over and out of my mind, if not my heart, and I could consciously pray for each person coming to the table. These were my best moments of worship each Sunday. Usually, because of the name tags and my use of worshipers' names during communion, I could remember at least the first names of new visitors as I greeted them at the door after the service. More than once, people told me that they came back to Saint Francis for a second visit because I noted their presence and remembered their names. You see, the values of this new church were being fleshed out in its first practices and traditions, and the benefits were readily evident.

C. Kirk Hadaway, formerly a researcher for the United Church [of Christ] Board for Homeland Ministries as well as a church-growth specialist with the Southern Baptist Convention, suggests that young churches have a "window of opportunity" for significant growth that may last for 10 or 15 years.[14] Why do new churches tend to grow more rapidly than older churches? It could be, Hadaway notes, that new churches are more flexible and open to change; growth-producing ideas can be put into practice; leaders are able to lead; rapid adjustments can still be made to changing circumstances; and friendship networks have not yet solidified, allowing for easy acceptance of new members.[15] Research conducted by Hadaway on Southern Baptist churches shows clearly how the age of a church affects its growth pattern. Only one in four Southern Baptist churches in his study organized prior to 1927 had growth in excess of 10 percent from 1981 to 1986, whereas nearly 68 percent of churches founded between 1972 and 1981 experienced this kind of growth.[16]

An old congregation's longtime members sometimes look back to the early stage of development as the "golden age" when the church was at its best. If the church is in decline, it is often to this idealized experience of church that members wish to return—a hope that can seldom be fulfilled. They remember the large youth group; the grand choral cantatas; the numerous births and baptisms; the weddings of first members' maturing children; the excitement of moving into the first church building; the young minister who knew everyone by name and who made regular home visits; and the perennially victorious men's softball team.

Stage 3: Equilibrium

After as little as a few years or as long as a human generation, stage 3 in the life cycle of a congregation usually begins. This is a leveling-out stage. Growth slows. New ideas are introduced less frequently. Traditions and practices become more routine and predictable. I call this stage *equilibrium*. It is a time when much of the congregational system's energy becomes focused on maintaining the status quo. The church has found its center. Although the church is not growing significantly during this stage of equilibrium, neither is it declining. Each year, enough new members join to replace those who leave or die. Enough money is contributed to meet the annual budget, including modest increases required to maintain ongoing programs. Facilities are more or less adequate for the needs of the church, and debt, if any, is low. Members are generally satisfied with the way things are, and they don't see the need to change much about the church's programs. Conflict tends to be low. Ministers come and go, but the church survives each transition, so long as the new pastor doesn't try to rock the boat by introducing too many new ideas.

It may not be readily apparent, but a congregation is at high risk during the equilibrium stage of the life cycle. This stage is not a seemingly boundless prairie. It is more like a mesa. Its top may be wide and smooth, but every edge of the mesa drops off precipitously to a plain or a rugged canyon floor. Living in equilibrium can have a slow-release narcotic effect on a church. Periodic highs mask the increasing sluggishness and dullness that mark the character of the church. These negative qualities are more readily apparent to newcomers than to longtime members. Robert Browning's oft-quoted poem "Pippa Passes" posits that "God's in his heaven—All's right with the world" (a notion that I find inane). This "hunky-dory" attitude too often characterizes equilibrium-stage churches: *God's in control in some distant place, and nothing needs to change around here.*

The older a denominational body, the more its congregations are likely to be found on the mesa of equilibrium, and consequently at high risk of shifting into decline (in size, as well as influence and effectiveness). These churches find their own techniques for maintaining their preferred identity, while at the same time suppressing growth.

The equilibrium phase of the congregational life cycle can be explained by a process that sociologist Max Weber (1864–1920) calls *routinization of charisma*.[17] Often, a young movement's traits are fundamentally shaped by its founding charismatic leader. A nascent movement, such as a young denomination or a new congregation, may initially operate with few rules and little hierarchical structure. The people gathered into the movement are captivated by the tutelage of the movement's founding leader, the movement's defining philosophy (or theology or ecclesiology), and the energies derived from their own, firsthand, life-influencing, if not life-transforming, experience of participating in the birth of the movement. But, as we will see, these effects are seldom sustained.

The early church described in the Acts of the Apostles exhibits many of the characteristics of a young, unbound movement. The apostles, energized by their recent firsthand experience of both the living Jesus and the resurrected Christ, preached the good news with great vigor, and many who heard their words "devoted themselves to the apostles' teaching and fellowship, to the breaking of bread and the prayers" (Acts 2:42). Many signs and wonders were performed by the apostles, and the people who saw them were awed. And "all who believed were together and had all things in common; they would sell their possessions and goods and distribute the proceeds to all, as any had need. Day by day, as they spent much time together in the temple, they broke bread at home and ate their food with glad and generous hearts, praising God and having the goodwill of all the people. And day by day the Lord added to their number those who were being saved" (Acts 2:44-47). These passages describe a group of people choosing to depart from the accepted behaviors of the day. They hear firsthand a life-converting message; they believe; they act in faith on their belief.

A new sect, like the Methodism of the late 18th century, was fundamentally shaped by its founder, John Wesley; and much of its early influence, growth, and success was derived from its unfettered capacity to carry an old gospel message into a rough-and-tumble frontier American setting where, along with other young Protestant movements, it would inspire an unprecedented religious revival. A new Methodist church, like Chestnut Ridge, founded in 1832, was fundamentally shaped by rugged circuit-riding preachers, like James Christie, who came into the wilderness of central North Carolina, preaching from a tree-stump pulpit sheltered by a brush arbor and illuminated by pine-knot torches and campfires. Christie describes the effectiveness of this unorthodox method of "doing church" when he writes:

> After preaching we invited such as were sincerely seeking redemption in the blood of Christ to come forward that we might all unite together in prayer to God for their deliverance; between thirty and forty accepted the invitation and we offered our petitions to God on their behalf, when one more was raised to declare that God hath power on earth to forgive sins."[18]

A new church-cum-movement, like Willow Creek Church, near Chicago in South Barrington, Illinois, is being fundamentally shaped by its founder, Bill Hybels, who is introducing new paradigms for church, such as seeker-sensitive worship, that break many of the canons that have defined the church for decades.

Yet, Max Weber points out that as a movement ages and its founder dies, *routinization* begins. It becomes the task of the movement's followers to continue the work of the founder. New converts become more distantly separated from the primal experience known by the movement's first followers. Structure and ritual serve to perpetuate former experiences. Germinal experiences become recalled experiences. Bureaucracy, characterized by an expanding hierarchical leadership structure, increasingly replaces grass-roots leadership and decision making. In a word, routine sets in, and a period of equilibrium begins.

Stage 4: Decline
Following a period of equilibrium in the congregational life cycle, a church can move into stage 4, *decline*. No longer capable of balancing losses of membership, participation, giving, or influence with the

counterweight of growth, the church slowly, or even rapidly, diminishes in strength. Decline becomes evident when the membership includes only one or two aging generational groups; budgets shrink or are not met; needed building maintenance is deferred; worship or Sunday school attendance declines; few professions of faith and baptisms take place; pastors' salaries are cut (or pastoral service is reduced from full-time to part-time); the same laity continue to serve as church leaders because no new leaders can be found; denominational mission funds are not fully supported; and long-standing programs are discontinued for lack of support. Such evidence of decline is often accompanied by congregational conflict, malaise, depression, blaming, scapegoating, anger, and withdrawal.

Initially, a church's active members may not realize that the church is in decline. Routine in a declining church can be a deceptive partner. Busyness often hides ineffectiveness. An outside observer, such as a newcomer to the community who visits worship for the first time, or a visiting denominational staff member, may readily see the signs of decline go routinely unnoticed by congregation members. As in the process of grieving, denial becomes a mechanism for members to cope with the increasingly obvious decline in their church.

A weakening tree branch can resist the forces of gravity for only so long. Likewise, a declining church eventually breaks from the pressures of its losses and its incapacity to sustain its former level of activity. This point marks the *realized* decline phase. Often characterized by a posture of crisis, this is a time of desperation for a church when it begins to acknowledge openly its inability to sustain itself. In denominational systems, a church in crisis often expects its parent organization to come to the rescue. Many denominational staff members know that they can expect to hear a statement like this from a declining church's pastor or the alpha leader: "For many years we have loyally supported the denomination's cooperative mission fund. Does your office have funds you can send to help us repair our leaking roof, replace our clogged plumbing, and pay our pastor?" For several decades, numerous aging denominations whose churches, in increasing numbers, are aging into decline have attempted to prop up and revitalize declining churches by sending funds to pay bills the churches are unable to satisfy. In spite of these gallant, though essentially misdirected efforts, many of these denominations have continued to decline in size and influence.

Despite the devastating effects of decline, churches are notoriously tenacious and do not succumb easily. Many will whittle away at expense-generating programs, facility needs, and personnel requirements to keep the church doors open. Members of nearly defunct churches do not handle thoughts of closure well. Once, the attorney son of one of eight remaining elderly members of a rural congregation came to the office of the area bishop and said in very direct language, "If you close my mother's church before she dies, I will sue you, this denomination, and anyone else I can find to hold liable for her unhappiness." The church was not closed by the denomination.

Stage 5: Death
Inevitably, some churches, once strong and vital in their ministries and influence, do die. Certainly, this is an unhappy occasion for the last members of the church and for those who have supported it in its years of decline. But, when viewed in terms of the lifelong benefits afforded by the church to its members and its community, its end does not have to be an altogether sad event. A good life's natural end is death. The same can be true of an organization or movement. God's genius is exhibited in the fact that both life and death are natural and necessary for the successful perpetuation of creation. We do well to remember the words of the writer of Ecclesiastes, who said: "For everything there is a season . . . a time to be born, and a time to die . . . a time to plant, and a time to pluck up what is planted . . . a time to break down, and a time to build up . . . a time to throw away stones, and a time to gather stones together . . . a time to keep, and a time to throw away" (Eccles. 3:1a; 2; 3b; 5a; 6b).

As a congregation (or denomination) moves from *birth* to *vitality* to *equilibrium* to *decline* to *death*, the insidious forces of routinization are at work, resulting in an entropy-like effect. In physics, entropy is defined as "the unavailability of a system's thermal energy for conversion into mechanical work."[19] In terms of the church, entropy is the unavailability of the church's original spiritual energy for conversion into a gospel-proclaiming mission. So the life cycle of a congregation is measured not so much in time (though there is often a correlation with time) as in terms of the distance it stands at any given time from its core spiritual purposes. Herein lies another clue to help answer the question, "Who's killing my old church?"

Movement from Mission to Survival

Writing in 1967, Donald L. Metz said, "If the church had been listed in the stock market over the past few decades, it would have been considered a booming enterprise. As an organization it has had an impressive growth, evident both in the enlargement of its membership and in the increasing amount of real property it controls."[20] If the church was like a bull market in the 1950s and early 1960s, it has been wrestling a bear in the decades since.

Metz was writing near the end of an extraordinary period of new-church and membership growth in the mainline churches from the perspective of a denominational executive with the former United Presbyterian Church. An astute observer of the church as a social organization, Metz describes in his informative book distinctions between what he calls "developing churches" and "developed churches." His explanation continues to help us understand the church today. "There is no single, clear watershed that marks the boundary between these two stages of the congregation's life," says Metz, "but the division is roughly indicated by the coincidence of several events: the leveling off of membership growth, the completion of most of the physical plant, and the attainment of a rather consistent financial support."[21] If Metz's categories of developing and developed church were put in the context of the congregational life cycle discussed earlier, the developing church lives on the rising side of the cycle heading toward equilibrium, and the developed church lives on the declining side of the cycle. According to Metz, the mark of a developed congregation is an idealization of the past, whereas for the developing congregation, there is a great idealism in looking toward the future.[22]

Metz postulates that a congregation is defined by two types of goals: *formal* and *survival*. Formal goals, he says, "are in reality the goals of the church (theologically defined), of which the congregation is the proximate empirical expression. These goals are derived from the Scriptures and other writings of which the tradition of the church is composed, are stated in explicit, though general, terms in the official documents of the denominational organization, and are interpreted and applied through the elaborations of the theologians, ministers, and church members."[23] On the other hand, survival goals are about maintaining a church's organizational integrity. Specifically, says Metz, "the survival goals are the recruiting and maintaining of members, the establishment of physical facilities, and the stabilization of a base of financial support."[24] It is easier to define and understand survival goals than formal goals. Survival goals are quantifiable and easily become the criteria used to measure the success or failure of a church: How many members have you received? Did you meet your budget goal? What buildings have you constructed? What programs have you accomplished? These become the questions asked by peers, observers, judicatory officials, and members themselves to judge the success of a church. Before formal goals can be used in a similar way, they must be put into concrete terms—a task often deferred, if not avoided altogether. Says Metz: "Members are able to understand what it means to get members, or raise money, or put up a building, but they are not so clear about the general mission."[25]

Both formal and survival goals are necessary. The church is a social system, set apart from other social systems and society in general by its particular and peculiar beliefs, purposes, and practices. Inasmuch as the church's formal goals help give definition to the church, its survival goals provide the requisite infrastructure allowing its members to live out their God-given mission. A problem occurs when survival goals become primary. Accomplishing these goals may bring a great sense of satisfaction to all involved, yet the *mission* of the church may fail for lack of at least equal attention. When a church's energies, time, and leadership are invested in developing the hard infrastructure of the church, and then maintaining these elements once they are in place, it does so at the expense of the primary purpose of the church. Says Metz: "[S]urvival in itself should not be taken as a primary goal. In fact, the congregation should be sufficiently dedicated to its formal goals that it is willing to risk not surviving as an organized unit."[26]

One might expect that once a developing church builds a strong membership base, creates adequate facilities, and underwrites its programs and staff needs with a suitable budget, it will move its focus to the more important formal, or mission, goals which may have long suffered neglect. But Metz notes that to the contrary, "Once the congregation is developed, it already has an established tradition and commitments to honor, and the nature of the survival goals has changed. Nevertheless, the congregation is stalemated in its efforts to effect a significant change in its orientation. Because of this stalemate and pressures for the maintenance of the congregation's organization, it essentially continues its service of the survival goals."[27] Similarly, if the church's leaders, who so ably led the church to accomplish its major survival goals, continue to lead the developed church, it is likely that they will continue to do what they know best—emphasize survival goal achievement.[28] Church leaders who have helped bring a church to a position where it is financially viable, and has a nice complement of helpful programs and an adequate cadre of volunteer leaders, are reluctant to yield their authority to others who do not share their view of the importance of survival goals. Minimizing risk to a congregation's survival and suppressing disagreement and conflict among members become hallmark characteristics of leadership in a developed congregation. The middle way—the safe ground— becomes the main way for the developed church. The notion of the sacrificial character of the church is abandoned for the sake of survival.[29]

Decline and Conflict

In addition to unprecedented new-church growth in the 1950s and early 1960s, the Methodists' North Carolina Conference experienced success in the creation and expansion of institutional ministries, including colleges, camps, and retirement centers. Successful major fund-raising campaigns led by the conference underwrote these capital expansions. Conference churches took great pride in their visible accomplishments. But by the 1970s and 1980s, few new churches were being organized; and colleges, camps, and retirement centers were working with diligence to fill their programs with participants, meet operating expenses, and reduce debt. The attention of the annual conference and its leaders moved from a creating to a maintaining mode. (At the same time, a capital-funding campaign was conducted to relieve an increasingly large unfunded pension liability for pastors serving eastern North Carolina congregations.)

In these later decades increasing pressure was placed on pastors and congregations to boost their support of a rising apportioned conference budget and to increase church membership. For a time, every pastor was required to prepare detailed membership reports (euphemistically called "evangelism reports"). Church members and pastors alike complained about the "number game" being played by the conference. Clergy morale took a precipitous dive. Lay support and trust of conference leadership and programming diminished noticeably.

Conflicts flared in congregations, at times sparked by such inconsequential matters as whether the minister should sport a mustache or whether the choir should wear robes in the summer months. Metz points out that survival goals provide a basis for unity within a developing congregation, helping to reconcile conflict about goals. When the primary survival goals are accomplished, conflict about differences in goal interpretation is more likely to emerge.[30] The manifestation of conflict often takes strange shapes, which, on first sight, seems to have little to do with the purposes of the church. In fact, focus on survival goals and an absence of clarity about the church's formal goals leave church members in a state of uncertainty and instability. Perhaps for the first time in the church's history, it experiences its own version of "fight or flight." Some members choose to stay and engage in battle over myriad issues, great and small; and others, as voluntary members of a social organization that has little leverage to keep them connected, choose to leave for greener spiritual pastures—or for no church involvement at all.

For six years, the founding members of Saint Francis Church and I worked diligently at the task of building church membership, raising adequate funds, and constructing a first building. By all measures, we were successful, and our survival goals were accomplished. Those were heady days, and for six almost blissful years, little conflict marred the complexion of this new church. But in the final days of completion of the first building, conflict surfaced, and most of it seemed aimed directly at the building committee and me. Why did the lights in the worship center look like pawnshop signs? Why was the countertop in the men's bathroom pink (a concern of three women, not men)? Our church logo had always included a Jerusalem cross, rather than the more traditional Latin cross, but one member insisted that she couldn't bear worshiping in our new worship center unless a "real" cross was prominently displayed. One member dropped by my office to let me know that he and a "group" of members were on their way to a meeting to suggest to my supervising district superintendent that I wasn't "spiritual enough." One member, the volunteer editor of the church newsletter, threatened to publish his opposing position to a recommendation being made about pastoral housing, since the meeting at which it would be discussed did not meet his schedule. Needless to say, our newsletter had no op-ed page. Reluctantly he agreed not to write the article.

Do the Right Thing

It has been noted that a church sometimes experiences a boost in membership growth and giving when it erects a new building and bears indebtedness as a result. For this reason, some churches have justified the expense of new building programs on the premise that the effort would lead to sorely needed new membership growth. Although they are not likely to define this phenomenon in Metz's terms, astute congregation members and pastors understand that focused attention on tangible, measurable, and achievable goals can temporarily energize and enliven a stuck and stagnated congregation. It is for this reason that developed congregations most often look to survival goals to pull them out of their malaise. What is less readily acknowledged is that the residual effect of survival goal achievement is often short-lived, leaving a church with more members on the roll, larger buildings, and more money, but little real accomplishment of formal goals such as spiritual growth, deeper prayer life or experience with God, maturity in discipleship, or committed efforts on behalf of one or more justice issues.

Alice Mann, an Episcopal priest and senior consultant with the Alban Institute, suggests, "Vital organizations tend to be clear and persistent (even stubborn!) about their fundamental reason for being but flexible about the means they employ to live out their particular calling."[31] It is precisely the opposite, a lack of clear purpose and an inflexibility, that plagues many churches today. In the mainline denominations, by age if not experience, most churches are, by Metz's definition, developed congregations. They have membership, leadership, buildings, programs, and money—perhaps just enough to maintain the status quo. But they show little evidence of commit-ment to formal goals. Perhaps this state of affairs should not be seen so much as an indictment of the church—the process is inherent to all social organizations—as it is an honest statement of a predica-ment from which they need to be extracted, even exorcised! Perhaps before the church in this plight can be freed to shift its primary focus to formal goals, confession of sin must take place. As the writer of 1 John says, "If we say that we have no sin, we deceive ourselves, and the truth is not in us. If we confess our sins, he who is faithful and just will forgive us our sins and cleanse us from all unrighteousness" (1 John 1:8-9).

If we love our buildings, our style of worship, our music, our pro-grams, and our traditions more than we love God, are we the kind of church we need to be? If we measure our success as a church by the size of our membership, the prominence of our leadership, the mag-nitude of our staff, the size of our budget, and the extent of our programming, are we fulfilling the mission God has given us? These are questions every church, new and old, needs to ask of itself—always.

Finding the Future

In his book *Death of the Church*, Mike Regele, Presbyterian minister and co-founder and president of Percept Group, Inc., writes:

> The institutional church in America . . . has built up many structures of self-dependence upon which it relies and into which it pours great resources. Yet these structures are failing. Like the individual who faces the faltering of his or her structures of self-dependence, the church is moving rapidly toward a moment of decision, a *defining moment*. It is a moment of definition because, whether we like it or not, the church in American culture is being redefined . . . *Simply, we can die because of our hidebound resistance to change, or we can die in order to live* [author's emphasis].[32]

Regele has been criticized for his book's title; nonetheless his point is clear that the church, as a collective body in the United States, is in trouble. The very fact that some people find the book title repugnant indicates how strongly a survival mentality dominates the attitudes of clergy and lay leaders today. Tradition-bound churches dominate the mainline scene. Jackson W. Carroll notes, "Because traditions are typically widely accepted—taken for granted in many cases—they have a heavy emotional and moral content that is given added weight by their special connection with the sacred. That is why they are so hard to change or ignore and why we often encounter severe conflicts (both externally and internally) when we do try to change them."[33]

In review, it is possible to see why old mainline churches and their parent denominations are having difficulty today.

- The once-dominant rural pattern of family-member perpetuation of church membership has been greatly degraded in most areas of the country.
- Old industrialized communities—where, to some degree, the rural pattern of family church membership was repeated for a number of generations in the 19th and early 20th centuries—have experienced their own demise, degrading the capacity for mill-village and town churches to survive.
- Sweeping demographic shifts from one racial, national, language, or economic group in communities have affected churches whose survival instincts and consequent resistance to change and risk have made it impossible to incorporate new and different neighbors into their memberships.
- The natural life cycle process inherent to churches and other social organizations is taking its toll on increasingly old and developed churches.
- A predominant focus in many churches on survival goals, not formal goals, as defined by Donald Metz, binds many churches to traditions and programs that are disguising the real mission of the church.

Blame for decline in the mainline churches has often been leveled at its purported liberalism and low commitment to evangelism ministry. But these are merely red herrings disguising the more likely causes of mainline decline in recent decades. As time passes, even more conservative and more intentionally evangelistic churches and denominations are at risk from many of the same causes of decline in mainline churches. The foes of the church are numerous, yet outside forces are not as treacherous as those lurking within the church itself.

The predicament of many declining churches today brings to mind John's description of the church in Laodicea: "I know your works; you are neither cold nor hot. I wish that you were either cold or hot. So, because you are lukewarm, and neither cold nor hot, I am about to spit you out of my mouth. For you say, 'I am rich, I have prospered, and I need nothing.' You do not realize that you are wretched, pitiable, poor, blind, and naked" (Rev. 3:15-17).

So long as local churches and aging denominational groups seek to define their futures from the successes of their past, they risk losing what is most valuable about the church. The church as an institution may survive in some form, yet the purpose of church as a vital community of faith may be obscured by attention to membership growth, fund-raising, building maintenance and the perpetuation of once-meaningful traditions. Even when solutions to the dilemma of decline are available, strong resistance to change prevents weakening, even dying churches from changing course.

Chapter Two

Are New Churches Better Than Old Churches?

Without deviation, progress is not possible.
—Frank Zappa

No one puts new wine into old wineskins.
—Jesus (Mark 2:22)

Improvisation is the ultimate human (i.e., heroic) endowment.
—Albert Murray

IF CHURCHES ARE NATURALLY PRONE to decline with age in the absence of clearly defined formal goals, is it likewise true that new churches are naturally inclined to grow and to be generally more effective than older churches? To begin our investigation of this important question, let's look at five churches in Greenville, North Carolina.

A Tale of One City

A university town in Pitt County, Greenville is a growing small city situated amid many rural counties in the state's coastal plain. Once driven by the production of cotton, tobacco, and peanuts, today the city's economy is built largely upon its university-related medical school and nearby pharmaceutical industries. The area of the city's primary ZIP code, 27858, has grown by 38 percent from 1980 to 2001 to a total of 41,240 residents. The number of households has grown in the same period by 46 percent. In the shorter term, between 1990 and 2001, the population increased by 35.3 percent. In 1980, the median household income was $13,228. By 2001, median income had climbed to $43,081.[1]

Greenville is served by four United Methodist churches. The oldest, Jarvis Memorial, was established in 1782, ranking it among the earliest of American Methodist churches. In 1952, St. James was founded; in 1962, Restoration, formerly called Holy Trinity, was started. It was closed down in 2002. Covenant was established in 1992. In 2002, Genesis Church was organized.[2]

Between 1982 and 1991, Jarvis increased in membership from 1,887 to 2,079 members.[3] In the same period, average worship attendance (in my opinion and that of many others in the field, the best measure of a church's size) decreased from 705 to 609. From 1991 to 2000, membership at Jarvis increased from 2,079 to 2,236. Weekly worship attendance remained stable, declining only slightly from 69 to 98.[4] St. James saw its membership increase between 1982 and 1991 from 1,374 to 1,872. From 1991 to 2000, membership decreased from 1,872 to 1,697. Average worship attendance increased in the first period from 356 to 503, and increased again between 1991 and 2000 from 503 to 644.[5]

Between 1982 and 1991, Restoration's membership grew from 246 to 376. Membership declined precipitously from 376 to 95 from 1991 to 2000. Average worship attendance grew slightly from 85 to 93 in the period 1982 to 1991, and declined between 1991 and 2000 from 93 to 71.[6] It seems likely that the dramatic decrease in membership at Restoration resulted from a decision to purge the church membership roll of inactive or nonresident members, since average worship attendance figures demonstrate only a modest decline over the same period. Cris Noble, Restoration's pastor before it was closed down in 2002, was assigned to begin a new church, called Genesis, elsewhere in the city. Organized only recently, Genesis averages above 100 in weekly worship attendance.

If worship attendance alone is used as a measure of membership activity in these United Methodist churches serving Greenville, then Jarvis experienced a decline in worship attendance of 13.62 percent from 1982 to 1991 and a much smaller decline of 1.84 percent from 1991 to 2000 with an overall decline of 15.18 percent. St. James

UMC saw an increase in worship attendance of 41.29 percent from 1982 to 1991 and an increase of 28.03 percent between 1991 and 2000, for an overall increase of 80.9 percent. Restoration had an increase in worship attendance of 9.41 percent from 1982 to 1991 and a decline of 23.66 percent from 1991 to 2000, for an overall decline of 16.47 percent.

Covenant, the fourth United Methodist congregation established in Greenville, was begun in 1992 without the benefit of a core group of members transferring from nearby churches. In its first 10 years, this church has grown to have a weekly worship attendance averaging more than 2,200, nearly 900 more than the combined total of the denomination's three older churches in the city. It can now, by nearly 1,000 worshipers, boast the largest average attendance of the conference's 846 churches.

Older Eclipsed by Younger

Here we have the example of a growing community whose older churches of one mainline denomination are quickly eclipsed in size by an upstart church from its own denominational family. The older churches have on their side the benefit of buildings, budgets, members, leaders, staff, programs, community visibility, and history. The new church has few, if any, of these assets to begin with, and asks little of neighboring churches. Yet the new church demonstrates an astonishing capacity for membership and attendance growth, far surpassing that of the other churches. It appears, in this example, that Covenant has been able to grow dramatically with negligible impact on the other three churches. Their patterns of decline or growth were already well established in the decade prior to the initiation of the Covenant congregation.

If this Greenville story were unique, it would be easy to dismiss as an isolated phenomenon driven by a charismatic pastor (but after only 11 years Covenant church is being served by its third senior pastor); an entertainment-oriented worship experience (which is not the style at Covenant); or the expenditure of extraordinary resources by denominational agencies to promote the church and its ministries (which has not been done at Covenant). To the contrary, this story is far from unique. All across the country, examples can be found of a new church becoming the strongest church in its community and in its denomination. Examples include Community Church of Joy (Evangelical Lutheran Church in America) in Glendale, Arizona; Saddleback Valley Community Church (Southern Baptist Convention) in Orange County, California; and Church of the Resurrection (United Methodist) in Leawood, Kansas.

Listen to the Experts

Fortunately, the case made by my anecdotal descriptions can be explained by people much more intelligent than I—scholars whose work dissects and describes the nature of the church from a more academic perspective. In this regard, I find especially helpful the work of sociologists and congregational experts C. Kirk Hadaway and Penny Long Marler.

Writing in June 1990 in the *Review of Religious Research*, Hadaway postulates that newer churches are more likely to grow than older churches, and that the relationship holds even when controlling for size of church and church setting.[7]

New churches, Hadaway notes, "not only add members when they come into a denomination, but they tend to grow faster than older churches. So the impact of new church development is cumulative. When denominations cut their levels of new church development, as many did in the late 1960s, they not only lose the potential growth of these new churches, they are also saddled with a progressively higher proportion of slower-growing older congregations."[8]

Precipitous declines in denominational size result from church closures, mergers, or disassociations from the parent denomination, and from national or regional church decisions to start few new congregations. Hadaway notes that in the United Methodist Church, "a reordering of denominational priorities and a 'top down' strategy of new church development resulted in a drastic drop in church starts which began in the middle 1960s"—leading to a decline in new church starts from 176 in 1961 to only 16 in 1971.[9] "The low levels of new church development in the past two decades have resulted in a progressively larger proportion of slower-growing older congregations in the United Methodist Church, and the effect of this trend will be felt for years to come," says Hadaway.[10] Lyle Schaller, noted observer of the church, states that denominations cannot rely on long-established churches to reach new generations of people, and that new congregations are the most effective approach to reach new people.[11]

Testing Hypotheses

Drawing from some suppositions about new-church development from Schaller and others, Penny Long Marler and Kirk Hadaway test three primary hypotheses in their essay "New Church Development and Denominational Growth" in the 1993 book *Church & Denominational Growth: What Does (and Does Not) Cause Growth or Decline* (Roozen and Hadaway, eds. [Nashville: Abingdon, 1993]). The hypotheses tested are:

1. Growing denominations have higher rates of NCD [new-church development] and an increasing average congregation size.
2. Growing denominations plant churches in areas that are "geographically favorable"—that is, in areas of high population growth, high in-migration rates, and/or unchurched people groups.
3. Growing denominations demonstrate *resilience* to the degree that they adapt to changing social conditions and sustain growth across congregational age, size, and location factors.[12]

Start Many New Churches

Marler and Hadaway, considering three mainline denominations—the Presbyterian Church (U.S.A.), the United Methodist Church, and the Lutheran Church–Missouri Synod—found that clearly, in periods of denominational growth, church-start rates were high, and in periods of denominational decline, start rates were low.[13] In fact, when all three denominations are combined, the correlation (Pearson's r)[14] between the number of new churches started and the rate of membership change was strong (.76).[15]

Build in Areas of New Growth

Likewise, Marler and Hadaway's study of several mainline denominations indicates that new churches tend to be located in places favorable to growth, lending credence to their second hypothesis. Noting that new churches are likely to be established in communities of newer and relatively more expensive housing, and with a higher proportion of college graduates, the authors observe that new churches are also more likely to be found in areas having a high proportion of multi-family housing, people who rent, and Hispanic and African American residents.[15] This final observation may be surprising to some, but the authors suggest that "new ethnic churches have allowed denominations to find new sources of growth and to ameliorate the embarrassing legacy of segregation in their histories."[16] They show that new churches tend to grow, regardless of their ethnic makeup, yet when a church is no longer new, non-Anglo congregations have better prospects for continued growth than Anglo churches.[17]

Adapting to Change

The third hypothesis tested by Marler and Hadaway proves to be credible as well. The most resilient denominations seem capable of adjusting to changes in their environments. Their capacity for adaptation and their determination and willingness to start new churches, in good times and bad, lead to growth, while less resilient denominational bodies experience decline. More resilient denominational bodies continue to display the qualities of a movement—more so than less resilient denominations. Resilient denominations' congregations tend to be either growing or declining, while few have been stable in the long term. Less resilient denominations tend to have higher numbers of churches showing neither significant growth nor decline. But what of the less resilient mainline denominations? Can they grow despite their condition? The authors offer a prescription: "Lacking the movement quality of the Assemblies of God and the conservative ideology of the Southern Baptist Convention (and LC–MS), new churches must result from organized bureaucratic efforts . . . the fortunes of these denominations lie in the direction towards which their efforts and resources are channeled."[18]

New Churches Are Volatile

Hadaway says that new organizations are inherently more volatile than older organizations. They are more likely to grow and more likely to die, but denominations can take heart in the fact that a larger proportion of new churches survive than do small businesses.[19]

My work for the North Carolina Conference requires me to lead in the creation of from three to five new churches each year. My fear of failing at this task is at times palpable, so on the wall just behind my computer monitor is posted a magazine clipping citing a 1999 U.S. Small Business Administration factoid; it notes that 52 percent of all small businesses don't survive beyond five years. Fortunately, in the North Carolina Conference, we're batting a much better average than that.

Why Start New Churches?

Twenty years of experience in the field of congregational development leads me to identify six compelling reasons for starting new churches.

- New people are more likely to join new churches than old churches.
- Old churches are moved toward renewal by the presence of new churches in their communities.
- Old denominations are renewed as the percentage of new churches in their total number of churches increases.
- New churches are more likely than old churches to be open to all kinds of people (inclusive of race, ethnicity, socioeconomic class, nationality, gender, etc.).
- New churches are more likely than old churches to call or receive female pastors, or pastors whose cultural background, race, ethnicity, or nationality differs from that of the majority membership.
- New churches find it easier than old churches to live out new models of mission and ministry.

People Who Join New Churches

New people are more likely to join new churches than old churches. A small east coast city is served by eight aged, seriously declining churches of the same denomination. The largest church, the denomination's mother church for the city's other congregations, has an average worship attendance of 200 people each week. When full, its sanctuary will easily accommodate 600. The smallest church has fewer than 50 people in worship. Essentially, each church in the group offers weekly worship, a few Sunday school classes, occasional fellowship dinners, and a variety of small-group ministries such as men's and women's mission and fellowship groups. The average age of the active members of these churches is judged to be above 55.

The city's population is much younger, having an average age of just over 30. It is a growing city, evidenced by the ongoing construction of new homes, new businesses, new schools, and new roads. Over the protests of the eight at-risk or struggling churches, a new church was started in the city with about 400 people attending its first Sunday worship service. Essentially none of this attendance came at the expense of the eight churches long active in the city.

Using Direct Mail, Phone Calls. This new church was led by Camille Yorkey, a new-church pastor who chose to use telephone invitations and direct-mail promotion to generate interest. She invited people she met—unchurched bankers, restaurant workers, and business workers—to come to the new church, and come they did. The church had little to offer but worship and the pastoral services of its minister. Meeting in rented space in a public school, the church was limited in its ability to offer nurseries for children or Christian education classes. For all but the three hours or so each Sunday when the school was available, and except for a small two-room office leased in an obscure business center, the new church was without physical space to conduct its ministries and to afford the visibility established churches usually have. The new church worked with a small and restricted budget, had few experienced leaders, provided little in the way of weekday or evening ministry activity, and supplied little more than the pastor for "staff services." Nonetheless, this new church began on its first day of worship with twice as many people gathered for worship as the largest nearby church from its parent denomination.

Again and again, this story is repeated wherever new churches are started. Though not every new church will begin with large numbers present, and despite the fact that not all new churches will survive, new churches have a demonstrable advantage in attracting unchurched people to participate in their worship, programs, and ministries. It's as though some hidden magnetism exists in new churches that isn't found in older churches. Older churches can be intentionally evangelistic and invitational in the same community as a new church and yet not get the same response. The older church may be visible in the community; may have a very attractive and accessible site and facility; may be a warm and welcoming community of Christian believers; may offer inspiring worship, complete with a moving sermon and rousing music; may have the best infant and toddler nursery in town; and may go the extra mile by offering coffee and freshly squeezed lemonade after the service to those who want to stay and chat a while. But an upstart new church meeting in a school gymnasium with no air conditioning can prove to be a more alluring venue and experience of church for newcomers.

This phenomenon is often as surprising to those who respond to a new church's invitation as it is to those who do the inviting. When a new church was begun in the golf resort town of Pinehurst, volunteers joined the pastor, Steve McElroy, in making numerous phone calls to identify and invite unchurched residents in the community to attend the church's first worship service. At the time, Pinehurst was the only incorporated municipality in eastern North Carolina with a population of more than 5,000 not served by its own United Methodist church. When one volunteer dialed a number, a young man answered the phone. The volunteer explained in a few words that she was calling about a new church that was being started; she asked whether the young man attended a church in the Pinehurst area. After a brief silence, he asked, "Who told you to call me?" The volunteer explained that everyone in Pinehurst was being called and that no one had asked, in particular, that he be contacted. Once again, he inquired, "No, really, who told you to call me?" By now it was becoming clear that he suspected that his churchgoing parents or in-laws had put someone up to making this call. But, again, the volunteer caller spelled out that she had a list of phone numbers and was merely working her way down the list and happened to reach his number. The young man relaxed and said: "You won't believe this, but my wife and I were married two years ago, just before we moved to Pinehurst. We both attended church as children and youth, but we haven't visited a church since we moved here. Just tonight, we were talking about how we should begin looking for a church." Still somewhat astonished by the timing of the phone call, he asked, "Are you sure no one told you to call us?" The young couple attended the first worship service and became vital leaders in the new church.

United Methodists might call this an example of what John Wesley called *prevenient grace*. This is the grace, God's love, that runs ahead of our conscious desire for God and leads us toward faith.

Diverse Attractions. Many more stories could be told of how effectively new churches attract new members. Seaside Church draws retirees who have moved to the community for golf, sun, and fishing; All God's Children Church attracts both low-income African American and white neighbors; Christ Church attracts affluent and highly educated university and business leaders; New Song Church attracts baby boomers and generation xers who like loud, body-vibrating band music; Iglesia Cristo Vive (Living Christ Church) attracts new Spanish-speaking immigrants who have moved north of the Mexican border for jobs—and all of these churches have attracted people who were not attending existing nearby churches whose ministries have much more to offer than the new churches they choose to attend.

So why do people choose new churches? Here are some explanations of this phenomenon.

The Lure of the New. For lack of a better way to explain it, *newness* itself seems to be a powerful attraction to people outside of the church. The same is often true for other new places. How often have you noticed that the newest restaurant in town outdraws all others for a while? Predictably, lines are long for a few months after the opening of a new restaurant. Perhaps those in line don't know whether the food will be good, the service adequate, the physical space comfortable, or the prices reasonable. But the newness of the place draws them to investigate for themselves. For an unchurched person, a new church may have this same appeal. Will it be different from other churches? Will it be more interesting than other churches? Will it be more meaningful to me?

Human nature causes groups of people to place themselves into circles of family, friendship, leadership, or control. Since most adults have learned through experience that older groups are predictably self-organized in this way, unchurched people may also sense that a new group is not yet subject to this cell segmentation, making it a place where time and opportunity will allow them to find a place for themselves. Therefore, the chance to form friendship circles and relationships will be high on the list of reasons that some people come to new churches, which are presumably open to newcomers, since everyone in the beginning is new to the church.

Some unchurched people in a new church community were formerly active in other congregations. They may have long desired to return to church life but have hesitated to return to their former church, fearing embarrassment at being asked to explain their long absence. The question may never be asked, but the fear may nonetheless be a powerful force preventing return. In some instances, a member's departure from a church may have resulted from a controversy, conflict, or disappointing experience. The conditions or circumstances that led to their departure may still exist. The former congregant may have been a cause of unhappiness to members who remain in the old church, or a source of disruption or conflict. The drop-out parishioner's reflection on these incidents may have led to remorse as well as a heavy burden of guilt. A new church becomes an open door for re-entry into a faith community that does not entail facing up to the fears, anxieties, or guilt associated with returning to a previous church home.

Most people understand, at least unconsciously, that new organizations are not as set in their routines as old organizations. Traditions are not yet fixed; space is available for more flexibility and experimentation in shaping the faith community's activities. Organizational and leadership structures are not unalterable. Some people drawn to new churches are said to be more like *pioneers* than *settlers*. For people with a pioneering spirit and attitude, the chance to be part of a new church venture, and to help give it form and shape and purpose, can be an exhilarating experience.

An Example to Older Churches
Old churches are moved toward renewal by the presence of new churches in their communities. Most mainline denominations were beset with large numbers of at-risk or declining churches for most of the last half of the 20th century. Consequently, much attention has been given by aging denominations to these churches. Attempts have been made to strengthen or "renew" these churches. Sizable grants and loans have been made available to some; mergers, relocations, and reconfiguration of multiple-church parishes

have been tried. Structured resources, like loans and grants developed for new churches by some denominational bodies in the 1950s, were redirected in the 1960s through the 1990s to benefit aging churches. At times, the denomination's best leadership has been deployed to save these flagging churches. Much attention has been given to judicatory staffing, priorities, and the availability of resources for what has variously been called redevelopment, renewal, or transformation ministry. Some denominations have focused their energies on major programs aimed at strengthening struggling churches. Campaigns and programs like the United Methodists' "Vision 2000" and "Growth Plus" and their more recent "Igniting Ministries" national media campaign have been mostly directed at aging churches, not new ones. It could be said that the whole church-growth movement, including much of what has been published by major religious publishing houses, and blueprints like Kennon L. Callahan's *Twelve Keys to an Effective Church* and Christian A. Schwarz's *Natural Church Development*, have mostly had in their sights the question of how to save the declining church.

It is the natural tendency for an organization, like an organism at risk, to turn toward measures ensuring self-protection. Much like musk oxen that strategically gather with haunches backed up and packed tightly together toward the center of a circle, heads and massive horns facing outward toward the predators who stalk them, old churches in decline take noticeable measures to defend themselves against the forces they perceive as contributors to their possible demise. For this reason, a great deal of resistance has been mustered in mainline denominations against efforts to rekindle a priority for new-church development. This resistance has sometimes come from the top down, from judicatory leaders and agencies. But more often the greatest antagonism toward plans for new-church development comes from pastors, leaders, and members of local churches.

The frequent reaction of nearby churches at the announcement of a new-church start in the neighborhood is horror: "A new church will kill our church." An insensitive response to those who voice such feelings is to suggest that it appears that congregants have been doing a good job of killing their church without the help of a new church nearby! Like their better-known cousins, the NIMBYs (Not in my backyard!), these NIMPA churches (Not in my parish area!) have more than once effectively blocked the creation of a new church in their community. Another frequent response to a new church project is to suggest that if the denomination were to give the old church the same amount of money as it plans to plow into land and buildings and salaries for a new church, then the older church could grow and be strong again. Again, a cynic might note that most existing churches have land, buildings, staff, lay leadership, income, and programs to offer, but without much growth to show for it. A third response to the arrival of a new church is for leaders of the old church to claim that the parish territory targeted by the new church for outreach belongs to them, not to the upstart congregation (suggesting that some kind of unwritten, intradenominational comity agreement exists). A real clod would remind the dying church making this argument that it has had the territory for a hundred years and perhaps it's time to let someone else have a go at it!

Why Established Churches Gain. Where numerous new churches are being started in mainline denominations, a most unexpected effect on nearby old churches can be observed. In many cases, not only is the old church not harmed by the new church—in fact, the old church becomes stronger than it was for years before the new start-up. Marler and Hadaway have shown that even in communities where megachurches are formed, the growth of smaller nearby churches and the advancement of new-church development are not hindered.[20] There are several possible explanations for this phenomenon:

1. New church efforts at recruitment of unchurched people frequently lead some people to visit established churches instead.
2. Members and leaders of the old church become more concerned about their church's future and image in the community, and therefore become more intentional about inviting unchurched friends, co-workers, family members, and neighbors to join them at church activities.
3. Invitational contacts by the new church often spur an old church's own inactive members to reactivate their membership in their former church.
4. Old churches often learn how to reach out to unchurched people by observing the tactics employed by the new church.

5. Old churches often add significant new ministry opportunities (such as additional worship services), using many of the same outreach methods utilized by new churches, which carry much of the same attractive appeal to unchurched people as does the startup of a new church.

When I became pastor at Saint Francis, I inherited a somewhat discouraged remnant of the original core group formed by the church's founding minister. About 20 adults seemed sure of their commitment to continue with the church, and it took about six months to recover about 20 more core group members who were more tentative about their commitment to the church. For half a year, no new visitors came to join us in worship. Once it seemed that the core group was adequately prepared to welcome newcomers, I suggested that we send out a series of invitational mailings to all of the 10,000 households in our community. We had been booted from our original school meeting location by an unenthusiastic principal, and our new worship site was hidden inside a residential neighborhood, its site largely unknown to anyone whose child did not attend that school. We had almost no physical or programmatic visibility in the community. The first mailing resulted in 75 new visitors. Needless to say, we were excited and encouraged about our prospects for survival. So far as I know, this was the first use of large-scale direct mail to recruit new members by any church in our denominational area. I received a number of phone calls as a result of the mailings. Some came from inquiring residents wanting additional information about our church. But oddly enough, a number of the callers were area United Methodists active in their own churches, but curious to know what we were up to in sending invitations to their members to visit our church. Well, that, of course, was not our intent; but it became evident that our mailings were perceived by some as a threat to their church's health and strength. In one case, referring to the use of direct mail *advertising* for our church, the caller flatly declared, "We Methodists don't do things that way!" Despite these protests, it wasn't long before the use of direct mail became the preferred medium for new and old churches of many denominations in our area for announcing the initiation of major new ministry programs. Today, in fact, some companies specialize in predesigned direct-mail services, supplying color-

ful cards and fliers and providing mailing labels and postal preparation services to accommodate churches of all ages and sizes.[21]

Helping Denominations Grow
Old denominations are renewed as the percentage of new churches in
their total number of churches increases. Hadaway and Marler conclude in their study of new church development that new churches
are a cause of growth in mainline denominations:

> For mainline denominations, we have shown that little growth has
> come from new churches in recent years, because these denomina-
> tions simply started so few. However, growth has been enhanced in
> those eras in which they have started many—even when controlling
> for period effects. So for the mainline, new churches are more a cause
> of growth than they are a symptom of growth. When these denomi-
> nations make the effort to start new churches, they tend to grow (or
> at least moderate their declines.) When they do not make the effort,
> they tend to decline.[22]

Denominations with a higher proportion of new churches tend to
grow more than denominations with few new churches, because
younger churches tend to grow more than old churches. For example,
in the Southern Baptist Convention, among its oldest churches (those
formed prior to 1928), 22.4 percent were shown by Hadaway and
Marler to be growing churches (increasing in membership over 10
percent in a five-year period), whereas 62.5 percent of its younger
churches formed between 1973 and 1982 were growing. The difference between the percentage of growing older churches and younger
churches was 34.8 percent to 48.8 percent for the Assemblies of God;
17.8 percent to 46.1 percent for the American Baptist Convention;
16.4 percent to 47.5 percent for the United Church of Christ; and
13.0 percent to 46.8 percent for the Presbyterian Church (U.S.A.).[23]
Evidently, the capacity of new churches to cause increased growth
diminishes with time, suggesting that sustaining the growth effect of
new churches on aging denominations requires an ongoing program
of new-church development.

This phenomenal relationship between the age of a church and its
rate of growth may offer the most important explanation for why
denominations rise and fall in membership. At their periods of greatest growth, denominations have been engaged in new-church

planting. Likewise, major membership declines are experienced when few new churches are begun. Between the Civil War and World War I, unprecedented numbers of new churches were created by numerous denominations. Lyle Schaller notes that in this period, the number of Methodist churches increased by 47,000. In contrast, during the 1980s United Methodists started fewer than 700 new churches.[24] In the UMC's North Carolina Conference, at least 513 churches were begun between 1870 and 1909. Only three churches were started there in the 1970s and 19 more in the 1980s.[25]

A second factor may be equally important in explaining the importance of new-church development by aging denominations. Despite an overall decline in membership in many denominations, the average size of congregations has increased, in some instances significantly, during the 20th century. New churches tend to have higher average membership numbers than older churches, and much of the increase in average church size can be attributed to bursts of new-church development in most mainline denominations at the beginning of the 20th century and again at mid-century. Schaller notes that between 1906 and 1988, the average number of members per congregation increased from 93 to 236 for United Methodists; from 149 to 258 for the United Church of Christ; from 132 to 252 for the Presbyterian Church (U.S.A.), from 132 to 235 for the Episcopal Church; from 95 to 395 for Southern Baptists; from 167 to 350 for the Evangelical Lutheran Church in America; and from 161 to 332 for the Lutheran Church–Missouri Synod.[26] (In some cases, names of merged denominations are used, although predecessor church bodies were in operation for part of the time period covered.)

A clear correlation exists in the UMC's North Carolina Conference between young churches and larger membership. In 2000, the average membership of 832 churches in the conference was 275 members. The average worship attendance of a subset made up of new churches started in the conference since 1953 was 442 members. Excluding the membership of these newest churches from the total conference membership makes the average membership of all older churches (those started before 1953) 257, making the younger group of churches 72 percent larger in average membership than the older churches.[27]

Membership Change

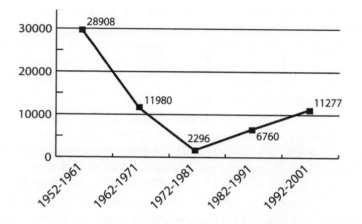

New Churches Started

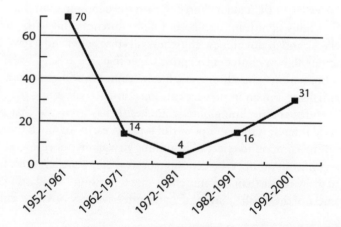

Figure 2: Membership Change Compared to
New Churches Started, 1952–2001
North Carolina Conference, UMC

In investment strategy, there is a concept called dollar-cost averaging. This theory suggests that if a person systematically invests a set amount of money in the stock market, say $100, every month or quarter without fail, then over time the declining stocks purchased will be offset by the gaining stocks acquired. Apparently, this effect is caused by the fact that your dollars are purchasing some stocks at a peak cost and some stocks at below their fair value, averaging out the risks involved in investing in the stock market. Since investing in stocks over the long term has proved to be a good way to increase wealth, dollar-cost averaging ensures that you are in the market with reduced risk of failure. The benefits of dollar-cost averaging include the discipline of regular investing and the reduction of risk associated with trying to guess when to buy and when not to buy. Your dollars purchase fewer shares when the market is up and more when it is down. In order to make dollar-cost averaging work, the investor has to be prepared to commit to the investment process over the long term.

We can see parallels between dollar-cost averaging and the idea that denominations should regularly plant new churches as part of a long-term strategy for growth. If it is true that younger churches tend to grow larger than older churches, then the denomination that regularly begins significant numbers of new churches is likely to grow as well. Although not all new churches will survive beyond a few years, and not all new churches will grow larger than the average size of the denomination's churches, enough new churches will grow to a substantial size and an impressive missional impact, offsetting the effect of failures and declining older churches. It has been said that compound interest is the most powerful force on earth. In much the same way, the compound effect of beginning new churches year after year in significant numbers by denominations—they generally grow faster and grow larger than old churches—has a profound and lasting outcome on the health, strength, and effectiveness of these church bodies.

A Welcome for All

New churches are more likely than old churches to be open to all kinds of people. A new-church pastor and I were riding in a car through the community where the church he was organizing was to be planted. As we rode through many diverse neighborhoods, the young leader said to me, "You know, we've prayed that many people will come to our first service; we've called more than 20,000 homes to invite unchurched persons to attend our first service; and we've sent thousands of pieces of mail telling people about our new church. You know that we've invited everyone in town to come, and that means that we've invited all kinds of people—black and white and rich and poor and educated and uneducated."

"That's good, isn't it?" I said.

"Oh, sure," said the pastor, "but what if they all come?"

I laughed and said, "You've done a good job, but I don't think they all will come."

"No," he said, "I don't mean everyone. Just, what if all kinds of people come?"

I knew what he meant the first time, but this time I again responded, "That's good too, isn't it?"

"Of course," he said, "but my fear is that I may not know how to minister to all kinds of people."

The pastor's concern demonstrates one of the challenges facing leaders of the church today. Regrettably, while many of society's institutions—schools, businesses, clubs—have become more and more integrated in their makeup (integrated by race or age or income level or educational experience), the church, on the whole, has lagged behind and remains one of the most segregated bodies in the United States. Consequently, few pastors have had a firsthand opportunity to learn how to lead diverse congregations and how to help them grow. He was not afraid that the church's first members would be diverse, but that he would not be up to the task of leading that kind of church. On the first day of worship, more than 360 people pressed into a gymnasium, giving birth to the new church, and they were as diverse as the neighborhoods from which they had come.

While nearby churches may remain resistant to being open to all kinds of people, quietly, perhaps, without saying that not everyone is welcome, new churches opened in the same community often begin with a membership reflecting the diversity of its neighborhood. Surely, it is a challenge for a new church to maintain this diversity, but quite often the new church is more intentional about taking steps to ensure that there is a place for everyone who comes, making the congregation into what is at times called a *mosaic* church.

Reconciliation Church, Durham, N.C., was started in a community where the population was nearly equally divided between white and black residents. Demographic studies of the community suggested that the area was already integrated, with neighbors of both races living side by side. Overall, the residents were equally well educated, lived in homes of comparable value, and worked at many of the same jobs. To start Reconciliation Church, a decision was made by the bishop to send out a team of two pastors to the targeted neighborhood—an African American senior pastor and a white associate pastor. This differentiation in roles was intentional, since it was believed that black residents might be more cautious about selecting a church from a denomination perceived to be a predominantly "white church." If led by a white pastor, or by co-pastors of equal status, it might be harder to persuade the black portion of the community that the church was truly a place where they would be welcome. Not only has this church successfully built an integrated membership from black and white residents; its membership today includes Asians and Latinos, as well as well as Africans, Latin Americans, Europeans, and so forth, who hold temporary or permanent U.S. residency status but remain citizens of their native countries. In contrast, three nearby churches of the same denomination have a total of only nine non-white members out of 1,731 baptized and confirmed youth and adult members on the roll.

The Homogeneous Church Theory. While some churches are an amalgamation of all of the groups represented in an area, some new churches attract more homogeneous groups of people, though people who are not typically reached by churches of the parent denomination. For example, it may be that the members of most long-established mainline churches today tend to be mostly white, middle-aged or older, in middle- to upper-income levels. When new churches are started by these denominations, it is not unusual for some of them to have a predominantly or exclusively ethnic-minority membership, a non-English-speaking membership, or a membership representing a lower socioeconomic class. Some new churches appeal to heavily tattooed bikers; some to young adults in their early 20s; and some to folk who are tuned into spiritual retreats, walking the labyrinth, and daily Eucharist.

The much touted and equally criticized church-growth movement's homogeneous unit principle[28]—which notes that people are attracted to people who are like them and that church memberships are made up largely of people who are drawn together because of what they have in common—is an evident and strong force that shapes churches as it does many other social institutions. New churches, like old churches, are not immune to the influence of this attribute of human nature. Yet new churches have a unique opportunity to live out another way to be church. Momentarily in the beginning of a new church's history, many of the ingrained barriers often present in older churches are nonexistent, giving the new church's first pastor and leaders a chance to form a new kind of church. New churches have frequently proven to be the breakthrough places where old norms of church membership and leadership have been broken down, reflecting the vision of Galatians 3:26-28: "For in Christ Jesus you are all children of God through faith. As many of you as were baptized into Christ have clothed yourselves with Christ. There is no longer Jew or Greek, there is no longer slave or free, there is no longer male and female; for all of you are one in Christ Jesus."

How often have a church's members found excuses and explanations to justify the closed nature of their church's membership? We've all heard the reasoning, and some of us have promulgated the myths and misunderstandings that have excluded some from membership in our churches. Do any of these lines sound familiar?:

"They are all Catholics, and they have their own churches."

"They wouldn't like the way we worship or the kind of music we sing."

"All black people go to church—and they go to their own churches."

"They are more liberal [or conservative] than we are, and they just wouldn't fit in here."

"Everyone around here is Baptist."

"We would never turn away anyone who wants to come and worship here, but we shouldn't have to change things to suit them."

Admittedly, new churches can be just as exclusive in membership as older churches. But more often than not, much of the paradigm-busting that opens the church to new models of ecclesial life happens first in new congregations, which are less entrenched by the effects of long-practiced routines and bureaucratization.

Openness to Atypical Pastors
New churches are more likely than old churches to call or receive female pastors, or pastors whose cultural background, race, ethnicity, or nationality differs from that of the majority membership. In the early years of my ministry as a pastor, I remember hearing stories about the disrespect, or worse, experienced by the first women assigned as pastors of churches in our conference area. Some were shunned by church members who boycotted worship in protest; some received veiled or even direct threats to their health and well-being; some were physically locked out of the churches they had been sent to serve. Such behavior by parishioners did not display Christianity at its best.

Likewise, I recall the questions raised when, after a long hiatus from church planting, our conference assigned women as some of the first pastors to begin new churches. Some said, "Women seem more suited to pastoral care and compassion ministries. Do you think a woman can make a new church grow?" Others said, "Do you think unchurched people will be attracted to a church led by a woman? Wouldn't a young, energetic male pastor interest more members?"

Although some women assigned to begin new churches in the conference have been more successful than others, the same has been true for male leaders. Not only have women started new churches well; some have given exceptional service as the clergy leaders assigned to replace founding pastors.

TV preachers who scream, cry, prance around a stage, beg for offerings, pump out pious platitudes, or sing sweet verses do not appeal to me. I would not be attracted to that kind of church, yet there is something I admire in them. Many of the churches I see portrayed are led by African American pastors, while their congregations are a blend of many races. Others are led by white pastors, and their congregations, too, are more integrated and are frequently much larger than most traditional mainline churches I visit. Many are led by female pastors, or by clergy couples displaying equal roles in worship leadership. Their churches seem to be attractive to the large and diverse live audiences in the auditoriums from which the services are televised. Often, I learn, these are newer congregations, and more often than not, they are not affiliated with any mainline denomination.

Why is it often easier for a new church than an old church to embody new patterns of ministry? The answer to this question may lie in the very nature of the church. Churches are emotional systems, according to Lutheran pastor Peter L. Steinke, and such systems are shaped by the forces of anxiety. Relationship systems are not necessarily harmed by anxiety, since anxiety can awaken a group to its need for change. But Steinke describes two types of anxiety. *Acute anxiety* occurs when our relationship system is shocked by a short-term crisis. A budget shortfall, the loss of a leader, or the destruction of a building by fire might precipitate acute anxiety. Given a little time, and some pain, acute anxiety is usually overcome without lasting detrimental effect on the group. It can even be beneficial if the experience leads the group toward positive transformation. *Chronic anxiety*, on the other hand, is habitual Steinke says, and becomes endemic to the group's life. Chronically anxious churches become obsessive about their beliefs and practices, and they attempt to impose their way on others. The anxiety of one person reinforces the anxiety of another as a vicious cycle—a pattern of anxiety-reactivity-rigidity-polarity-anxiety is perpetuated. A church like this can become intolerably inflexible in what it believes is the right way to "be church." The greater the anxiety, the greater the resistance to change in such a church.[29]

Although it is difficult for a chronically anxious church to break free from its rigidity to accept new ways of being the church, it is rather easy for a new church to begin free of the constraints of an anxiety-bound system.

An old-system church may refuse to receive a pastor because she is a woman or is from outside the membership's primary racial group or nationality—arguing that this minister is an untenable solution to the parish's leadership needs; that the lay officers and leaders have never done it that way before, and they don't plan to do it that way now; or that the proposed clergy leader is theologically unacceptable.

In a new church the primary issue is more often focused on such questions as "Has she done good work elsewhere?" or "Can she preach a good sermon?"

It is my opinion that many older churches are victims of chronic anxiety, whereas most new churches enjoy an absence of anxiety in their initial years, or experience acute anxiety at worst. This difference alone may explain why some older churches are resistant to change and why many newer churches are open to experimentation with new forms and practices of ministry.

It is possible that new churches believe that they have less to lose than long-established churches, whose traditions have become embedded in congregants' collective psyche; thus the newer churches are willing to take more risks. Judicatory leaders may, in fact, choose to create a new church and to assign a founding pastor who has nontraditional views about the church, because these leaders believe that it is more possible to begin something different in a new church than in an old church.

Not Your Mama's Church

New churches find it easier than old churches to live out new models of mission and ministry. New Song Church is way beyond rock 'n' roll in its style of music. This church *just plain rocks.* Its preacher is not tethered to a pulpit, and with head-mounted microphone and guitar in tow, he roams the stage (nothing that could be called a chancel here), leading the enthusiastic congregation of young and old and professional-class and working-class members through an hour or more of praise and spiritual instruction. To invite its first members, the church used a cable TV ad depicting a long-haired, milk-drinking young man jumping from a bridge with a bungee cord—which, unfortunately, he failed to attach to anything but himself! As a thud and a muffled groan are heard accompanying the image of an empty bridge railing, an announcer asks, "Got Jesus?"

The church's first building is a unique contemporary structure made by pouring concrete into an inflated dome-shaped form. No gothic arches, stained glass, or colonial columns here. This innovative congregation is United Methodist, and as I've said to friends more than once, "This is not your mama's church." In spite of, or perhaps because of, its out-of-the-box style and its sense of evangelistic and mission purpose, this new mainline church is reaching hundreds of people through its various ministries each week. Its ministries complement those of more traditional churches nearby without competing for the same potential members. Its innovative undertakings have caused it to reach and serve a constituency that, for the most part, had not previously found its way to the more traditional churches in the community.

In east Tennessee in the 1940s, a young church was outgrowing its first sanctuary, and its leaders resolved that a new worship center was needed. But amid the planning for the new facility, one heroic person suggested that the church should build an indoor swimming pool instead of a sanctuary. The extraordinary suggestion came complete with a rationale: After World War II, the small mountain city was filling up with young families and their children. If the church were to build an indoor swimming pool, and if a staff person were added to organize and lead youth ministries related to the aquatic facility, the church would provide a valuable ministry, and new families would be attracted to the church. Then it would be easier to build the kind of sanctuary required for a growing church. Remarkably, this church delayed the construction of its sanctuary, built an indoor swimming pool, and became known as the church that cared about youth. The pool was closed only a few years ago, and today the church has a magnificent sanctuary and an active and vital congregation.[30]

More and more, new churches construct first facilities to accommodate multiple activities in every room. Many include showers and sleeping areas to provide housing for visiting mission teams or homeless families. In worship areas, drop-down projection screens are more typical than stained-glass windows. Worship is offered two or three times each week, not once, and in some churches, never at 11 A.M. on Sunday. Sunday school is abandoned as the primary locus of Christian education, and small-group ministries offered throughout the week become the essential source of discipleship training.

Innovation and the adoption of new ideas and the acceptance of new people is not always easy in old churches. A small rural congregation's pastor discovered that near the church were numerous low-income families, mostly living in mobile homes, whose households included many young children. Meeting these families, she learned that quite a few of these families had no church relationship. On Sunday afternoons, she set out to begin a family ministry activity which included the creation of a children's choir and a family fellowship time. Several families and their children began coming on Sunday afternoons, and a few ventured into worship each week, as well. It could be said that the pastor was long on vision for mission and short on her understanding of the nature of the "family church." Her work was driven by a sense of what seemed right for the church to do. Members of the church saw her work as threatening to the way things had always been, or at least to the way they wanted them to be. Despite the church's small and declining membership and members' high average age, it became evident that most members would rather die than allow these "outsiders" to "take over our church." Locks were changed on doors without the pastor's knowledge; water to the church was cut off during Sunday afternoon activities; complaints against the pastor were lodged with her denominational supervisor. Today, this church, ironically named "Savages," after one of its founding families, endures with about 20 people gathering for worship each week.

Resisting Change. Naturally, resistance to change is strong in all of us. We all tend to find our comfort in certain customs that remain predictably the same. I sometimes have fun with members of congregational groups by asking them about their "favorite seats" in worship, to point out how little habits like sitting in the same pew every Sunday can become a barrier to newcomers who don't see the invisible "reserved" signs scattered throughout the sanctuary. I then talk about more important issues that are affected by the barriers we put up with our resistance to change—such as reluctance to recruit newcomers for leadership roles; failure to welcome people into our church family "because they are not like us"; blindness to the truth that the church's mission is broader than taking care of its own members.

New churches can easily succumb to the same dynamics that bring rigid, inflexible attitudes to some older churches. Traditions, practices, and rules can become fixed informally, but almost permanently, in a new church in its very first years. It may be impossible to point to the meeting when such things were decided, and to identify one or more culprits who led the charge toward fixing certain traditions as "the way we do things around here." But often, a new church has a gratifying opportunity to be innovative in deciding how it will "be church" in a way seldom possible in older churches. In turn, new churches become, in a sense, the R&D (research and development) division for a denomination. New ways of being the church discovered in new congregations often find their way into older parishes whose members are able to break through the rigid constructs of an anxiety-bound system. The cumulative effect of this reorienting process in new and old churches, in denominations whose mission includes starting many new churches, can enhance the health and vitality of the parent denomination as a whole.

New Churches Are Like Jazz

If old-style churches are like classical symphonies, then new churches are like jazz. Jazz historian Albert Murray says, "When you see a jazz musician playing, you're looking at a pioneer, you're looking at an explorer, you're looking at an experimenter, you're looking at a scientist, you're looking at all those things because it's the creative process incarnate!"[31] Jazz pianist Jonny King suggests, "Whereas written music for classical performers indicates every note and rhythm the instrumentalist is supposed to play, a jazz lead sheet is a much more Spartan road map. The performer, in a sense, has to fill in the musical blanks."[32]

Jazz, in its origins, is a uniquely American form of music (not to ignore its African roots). One of its hallmarks is improvisation. It is a mistake to think of improvisation in jazz as an extempore act, for it is less about a lack of preparation and more about the freedom to go beyond the rules directing other forms of music. Murray notes that improvisation does not mean "'winging it' or making things up out of thin air. The jazz musician," he says, "improvises within a very specific context and in terms of very specific idiomatic devices of composition."[33] King suggests that jazz improvisers draw from the past but speak to the future. "Jazz improvisers," he says, "start with and draw on a common, shared body of musical ideas and expressions that have evolved through the years, although individual artists reinterpret these musical concepts in their own voices."[34]

Perhaps nowhere in jazz is the character of improvisation more recognizable than in the part of a performance call the "break." The break is the place where individual musicians are given the liberty to disrupt a tune, breaking its cadence, changing its course for a while, carrying the tune as far away from its roots of rhythm and harmony

as can be imagined without totally breaking it apart. Murray describes
the break as a jazz tune's "moment of greatest jeopardy" and its "moment of greatest opportunity."[35] In a way, during the break, the musician is composing on the fly. He or she is not totally disconnected
from the piece being played, and the individual always comes back in
to join the group. But when let loose to play, the soloist challenges
the constraints of composition, performing experiment after experiment with the raw material of notes and rests elicited from strings or
keyboard or horn. This apparent unpredictability in jazz makes some
listeners uncomfortable and can make it an intimidating form of music
for those accustomed to a score being played as written from the first
measure to the last. Some who don't like it flee from it; others scorn
it for straying too far from what they consider the sensibilities of
good and proper music. But the essence of jazz is its unpredictability,
and without this element there would be no challenge to it and the
music's creativity would be quashed by its regularity. There are ground
rules guiding jazz, and every artist playing an improvisational break
is subject to them. But the beauty of jazz is the license it gives to have
fun within these rules, to test them and stretch them to their creative
limit.

Playing jazz is not for the fainthearted. A jazz player exhibits courage, endurance, and steadfastness when carrying a tune to its maxi-
mum expression and back again to a place where it is grounded in the
realities from which it has arisen. When a jazz musician ventures into
the open space given to the break, he has to be prepared to get lost in
the journey, to travel around an unknown country looking for his
way out, and upon finding the gate again, to leap out of it into the
relative safety of the band, which has all the while been hovering
nearby and trying to keep up while maintaining the foundations of
the tune. The rewards realized by facing the uncertainties and risks of
the improvisational method when playing jazz can be great. Outspo-
ken writer and critic Stanley Crouch says, "The success of jazz is a
victory for democracy, and a symbol of the aesthetic dignity, which is
finally spiritual, that performers can achieve and express as they go
about inventing music and meeting the challenge of the moment."[36]

Even more challenging in jazz is the act of group improvisation.
Jazz artist Bill Evans states, "Aside from the weighty technical problem of collective coherent thinking, there is the very human, even

social need for sympathy from all members to bend for the common result."[37] Mobility, flexibility, cooperation, and concession become key words in the parlance of jazz. Jazz is an art both of the individual and of the group. A player carrying the break is never *not* a part of the group, yet the group concedes for a while its collective role, allowing the individual player enough creative space to enrich the tune and to enhance the result they are all aiming to achieve.

Tradition and the Improvised Church

In their parent denominations new churches are like the break in jazz. They are the places where improvisation on the themes of church most frequently occurs. Often led by one person—maybe the founding pastor—change (improvisation) requires the participation and cooperation of others as well. Much of the experimentation in new churches is disconcerting to members and leaders of the parent denomination, who have become accustomed to predictable ecclesial patterns. This is an age-old problem precipitated whenever the church is confronted with challenging new ideas. Jesus was criticized by Pharisees and scribes for welcoming sinners and eating with them (Luke 15:2). Peter was rebuked by members of the circumcision party for going to Gentiles and eating with them (Acts 11:3). A pastor friend of mine was reprimanded for using an overhead projector in his church's sanctuary when teaching the congregation new songs. I was admonished for offering a Sunday afternoon worship service in Spanish for migrant farmworkers. A new church lost members when pews and stained glass were omitted from its sanctuary building plans.

Harking back to the days of American frontier religion, we can see how the church used innovation in its conveyance of the gospel to capture the attention of people in emerging pioneer communities. Using camp meetings, lay preachers, and hymns sung to popular tunes, for example, the church brought thousands to the fold of Christianity. Were these unorthodox methods any less radical in the eyes of the traditionalists of that day than are the methods employed today by new churches? Perhaps not. The methods of John Wesley and the founders of today's other mainline denominations were surely perceived by some in their time to exceed acceptable boundaries, evidenced by the harsh criticisms and persecutions laid on them and their followers.

It is a mistake to think that what new churches offer in the way of improvisation in their approach to ministry is done without preparation or consideration of the foundational beliefs of the church or acknowledgment of the historic underpinnings of the tradition they represent. Close inspection usually reveals that underlying the innovative practices of new churches are an understanding and recognition of their "very specific context," as Albert Murray puts it. Like jazz musicians, new churches recognize the value of the past while seeking to pose the gospel in language and practices that speak to the future. A new church knows how to differentiate between acts of preservation and acts of transformation. A preservation-minded church tends to focus on its past, its membership, its programs, its budgets, its traditions, and its buildings. A transformation-minded church tends to focus more on the present and the future, its community, people who attend no church, and the need to bring positive change to the world.

I am not suggesting that every new church is successfully improvisational, nor am I suggesting that every old church is stuck in the mire of preservation for preservation's sake. But in general, new churches tend to have more capacity to play the "break" in aging denominations. Theirs can be an epiphanic role, manifesting God through their ministries in new, sometimes shocking, and even disconcerting ways. And without the benefit of the break, as in jazz, the church may not fully express what God desires it to be. Some people argue that jazz without the break is not really jazz. Perhaps in the same way, the church without new churches is not fully the church.

A Degree of Conflict

Albert Murray's sense that the jazz break is a moment of both risk and opportunity applies to the new church as well. A new church, its pastor, and its leaders risk transgressing the limits of a legitimate expression of the church. New churches are more likely to do this than old churches. The very fact that new churches tend to be given liberty to try new things, to express the gospel in new terms, and to make use of new media for this expression, allows them to stray far from the traditions that define the church. An old church tends to have built-in constraints that are hard to breach. On the one hand, an old church might tend to reside on one extreme of a polarity where rules and traditions and expectations allow little room for improvisation; on the other hand, a new church might reside on the other extreme of the polarity where too many rules and traditions and reason itself seem to be ignored. A denomination having both constrained and unrestrained churches (perhaps epitomized by the oversimplified dichotomy of old and new churches) is more likely than others to be a healthy denomination, because these two strong forces will tend to modify the extreme expressions of the church at either end of the polarity.

Alban Institute senior consultant Gilbert Rendle, in his book *Leading Change in the Congregation*, defines conflict as "two or more ideas in the same place at the same time."[38] The presence of many new churches among the ranks of a denomination's numerous old churches is bound to create some degree of conflict. This kind of tension can be one of the best things ever to happen to an aging denomination. It can also precipitate a healthy dose of what Peter Steinke calls "acute anxiety" within a denomination's churches. New churches can be like the irritating grain of sand that, though surely a nuisance to an oyster, leads to the production of a pearl of great beauty and incredible value.

Quitting the Cult of Preservation

A denomination that does not include new-church development as a mainstay of its strategy for spreading the gospel increasingly finds itself living on the side of preservation, not transformation. Its churches become increasingly settled and comfortable. Only the threat of their demise seems to awaken these churches to the need for change. If few new churches in a denomination are "playing the break," showing creativity and innovation in their approach to sharing the gospel in contemporary ways for contemporary people, old churches are deprived of examples of how to be more improvisational in their own approach to doing ministry. New-church development must not be seen as a programmatic fix for ailing denominations. A special four- or five-year denominational priority for new-church development will not suffice. Instead, new-church development must be viewed systemically as part of an ongoing strategy of outreach. Not only do new congregations have a tendency to be more effective in reaching people outside the church, they can awaken the sleeping giant at rest within denominations increasingly mired in old routines.

Are new churches better than old churches? Certainly, new churches can be good at many things; new churches are particularly important to old denominations. But they are "better" than old churches only because they are necessary for the health of a whole denomination.

Chapter Three

Franchise or Faith Community?

The church is a colony, an island of one culture in the middle of another.
—Stanley Hauerwas and William H. Willimon

It don't mean a thing if it ain't got that swing.
—Duke Ellington

Swinging is the elegant response to chaos.
—Albert Murray

IF MAINLINE DENOMINATIONS TAKE UP the task of planting large numbers of new churches, will these be authentic communities of faith, or will they be franchise sites perpetuating many of the bad behaviors of aging judicatory bodies? How this question is answered in the first decades of the 21st century is of ultimate importance to the future of the American mainline church.

It appears that most new mainline congregations today are being initiated by denominational offices (like mine) or staff (like me) and not so much by sponsoring congregations or by grass-roots groups of spiritual seekers. There may be several reasons why this is the case, including the desire of mainline denominations to use new-church development as a program to abate their losses in membership, income, and influence; denominational leaders' efforts to maintain a franchiser/franchisee relationship with member churches, and thus to maintain a level of control over the form, practices, and financial resources of the new churches; a lack of interest among existing churches in becoming sponsors because of their sense of insecurity about their own strengths, their fears that new churches will diminish their own capacity to tap into denominational resources, that they may lose the attention of judicatory leaders, or that they will lose their perceived position of influence and prestige in the denomination's region.

Can the Mainline Improvise?

If most new mainline churches are started by leaders who think this way, how can new churches started by denominational offices be "improvisational" churches freed to experiment with new modes of being an authentic church? Will they be so constrained by the parent denomination that they will merely perpetuate the tired forms of the past?[1]

People who participate in mainline congregations today probably feel that they are part of close-knit communities of friends and acquaintances. If we examine these communities, however, we might find that they are not always distinctively *Christian* communities. The array of beliefs among these churches' members is myriad. Members of these churches may be more at ease describing the responsibilities of membership (e.g., attendance, prayer, financial giving, service) than what it means to be transformed beings whose lives are characterized by Christlike morality, justice, and mercy. And that observation leads us to the question, What is the church?

How Christian Are Our Values?

Perhaps the vitality characteristic of young spiritual movements that was seen in mainline denominations when they were young has been lost as these denominations have aged. Church members who have become comfortable with the mainline church as it has been might appreciate the fact that they are not being asked to live out distinctively Christian values, either as individuals or as members of a faith community. Members' high level of comfort makes it difficult to dislodge a congregation from spiritual malaise. Likewise, many influential mainline leaders are comfortable with the shape of the extant church. They may have known nothing else, and I suspect they feel reassured or justified in their understanding of the church when they see new churches following old patterns. If these leaders impose all their values upon new-church pastors and members, little will be gained by planting new churches. For this reason, the mainline needs new churches whose leaders and members are free to follow new pathways in their search for what it means to be the church.

Although I dislike the isolationist-sounding term to describe the church, *Christian colony,* proposed by Duke Divinity School's Stanley Hauerwas and William H. Willimon,[2] I do agree with the fundamentals of their argument that a church's people should stand apart representing sharply focused values in a devalued world. In contrast to the aims of the *church growth movement,*[3] and those who promote a stripped-down approach to church characterized by *seeker-sensitive* worship,[4] a church taking seriously the task of living as a peculiar Christian community may, in fact, repel some from membership because of its distinctiveness and the demands of participation. Old churches have difficulty breaking away from Spirit-quenching attitudes and traditions; will new churches manage to distinguish themselves as Christian communities? I think the answer to this question can be *yes.*

Improvisation and Inclusiveness

In the South—and I suspect this is true in most of the country—the church lags behind almost every institution in racial inclusiveness and the elimination of racist attitudes within its membership. The contrast between how many old churches and some new churches approach this issue illustrates how new churches sometimes find it easier to improvise when enacting what it means to be the church today.

An African American pastor friend told me of a discomforting incident he had while attending a spiritual-life retreat. Shortly after he checked into his quarters, his roommate, who was white, entered the room. The roommate's look of surprise and perplexity were evident to my friend. Stumbling about for something to say, the white roommate, a layman, quickly made his excuses and departed, explaining that he would be sleeping at home, commuting each day to the retreat site. Perhaps some circumstance other than bald racism led this man to change his plans, but I doubt it. This example of one man's incapacity to overcome ingrained prejudice is indicative of an attitude that is pervasive in much of the church today. The church often finds itself similarly uncomfortable when it is faced with opportunities to be Christian and to be the church that fall outside its comfort zone. Fright leads to flight, and the church's people fail to be the church.

A Church with Core Values

In contrast, Reconciliation Church in Durham, North Carolina, introduced in chapter 2, is a new congregation whose name is drawn from, and its core values as a Christian community derived from, the text "All this is from God, who reconciled us to himself through Christ, and has given us the ministry of reconciliation" (2 Cor. 5:18).

Located in a middle-class suburban community whose population is roughly divided half-and-half between African American and white residents, this church was begun with two pastors, one black and the other white. The church's mission statement says:

> We are a Christian community that seeks to intentionally include all races and all cultural backgrounds. Our mission is to embody God's ministry of reconciliation through our practice of worship, devotion, compassion and justice.

Lawrence Johnson, the African American half of the pastoral team for Reconciliation Church, relates his childhood experience of growing up black to that of leading this unique church. Says Johnson:

> As a child I lived on a reservation. Each day I would ride the bus to school with other children: Native Americans, blacks, and whites. After an incident on the bus one day, the school was divided and we were all separated. We rode separate buses to school, the whites on one bus, and the blacks and Native Americans on another, and now a large fence divided the school. When we went outside to play during recess, we would reach our hands through the fence to our friends on the other side. Since that time, I have always wondered why we can't work together, especially those of us who call ourselves Christians. I am excited about leading a congregation that reflects the diversity and beauty of all God's children.[5]

The late C. Eric Lincoln, an African American and an eminent church scholar, was a charter member of Reconciliation Church. In a sermon preached from the church's makeshift pulpit in an elementary school gymnasium, Lincoln said:

> It takes courage to love. We have walked on the moon, but we have not walked with each other. We make ourselves intimately comfortable talking in chat rooms with total strangers on the other side of the world; but we don't talk with the people next door or down the street. . . . This new millennium could well become the most stressful era in our history as we try to avoid "relating" to the increasing awareness of God's other children who have a legitimate share in the bounty of good things with which he has blessed America. Are we ready to open up our hearts and minds to these new challenges, these new opportunities to love? Do we have the courage to try?[6]

Opponents of Inclusivity

Eric Lincoln's challenge to have the courage to love is shown in the story of another new church faced with the bedevilment of prejudice. A few remnant members of a discontinued all-white church came along with a newly named pastor to begin a church called Good Shepherd. For the most part, the church's first members were drawn from its new neighborhood, which included a rainbow mixture of white, African American, African national, and a panoply of other residents representing many nations from around the world. Worship on Sunday, conducted in the lower level of a neighborhood business complex, acknowledged the richness of the cultures represented in its young membership through its music, hymns, and languages employed. On Thursdays, evening worship was attended principally by adult residents of several nearby group homes lodging mentally and physically disabled people. With the patience of Job, worship leaders and mentally able worshipers helped others learn the Lord's Prayer, a single word at a time each week.

Not everyone in Good Shepherd's neighborhood appreciated the course of its mission. Founding pastor Mark Lykins relates his experience this way:

> As a core group of leaders began with Bible study in [our] living room, we began to realize that God was calling us to start a congregation

that intentionally reached out to *all* of God's people. As we put this belief, of reaching out to "all people" into action, we became a community of faith from 17 different countries. . . . While we were thrilled to see such a wonderful blend of people, cultures, races, and nationalities come together, some people in the community were not so pleased. We began running into difficulties purchasing land. Our church building was broken into on several occasions although nothing was stolen; only a rebel flag was left just inside the front door. Then, harassing phone calls began; bricks were thrown through the windshield of my two cars; and our two children were approached and told not to go to their parents' church anymore.[7]

During an attempt to purchase land for the church's first building, Good Shepherd encountered many vocal opponents to this church's presence in their community. Lykins and his members began to suspect that some of the most insidious antagonism was coming from people associated with the Ku Klux Klan. Lykins describes a meeting with county commissioners for review of their site-development plans:

During the meeting, one after another went to the microphone, telling one lie after another about why we, as a church, were wanting that property, about me being a cult leader, about them being afraid that I was "going to train the church members to kick-box" their front doors in and "rob" them. [The church hosted a Tae Kwon Do ministry for youth outreach.] They said, "This is not a normal church—why, normal churches don't have all these different kinds of people in them!"[8]

Indeed, this was not a "normal" church. And Lykins was right about Klan opposition to his church's mission.

Two-and-a-half years after the break-ins and other incidents, Good Shepherd's pastor was participating in a spiritual life retreat in North Carolina. He presented a talk on *justifying grace* on a Friday afternoon. That evening, as he and a friend sat talking on the front porch of the retreat camp, one of the "pilgrims" on the retreat came over on his way to bed. He looked at Lykins and said, "I've been trying to figure out where I know you from for the last two days. I know you, but I can't place you."[9] Then he told his listeners about how he had been in the Klan and how he had given his life over to Christ a year and a half ago.

Lykins says:

My friend and I were moved by his testimony and intrigued by his experience in the Klan. I chuckled and said that I had some Klan experience myself. He asked if I had been a Klan member, too. I said, "No, I was on the receiving end of the Klan." I then told him a little about my experience at [Good Shepherd]. He asked me, "Did you have some bricks thrown through your car windows? Were you broken into and rebel flags left?" When I told him yes, he began to shake, and tears formed in his eyes. I asked him, "How do you know all this?" He said, "I was the one who organized all that against you."

As I stood there looking at him, hurting so badly from the guilt of . . . what he had done to me, my family, and the church members, I turned to him and said, "I have every right to punch your lights out for what you did to me. But because I have been forgiven by God . . . in the name of Jesus Christ, I forgive you! And you are now my brother!" We embraced and cried while the other men on the Walk clapped and began to sing: "Sing Alleluia to the Lord."[10]

Making Abnormal Churches

These stories imply that racism is a problem in the church. Undoubtedly the church's imperfections are not restricted to racism. (The church can be accused as well of apathy toward people in need, a poor record of environmental stewardship, theological narrow-mindedness by liberals and conservatives alike.) But at least in the southern church, nothing illustrates more clearly than the manifestations of racism how "abnormal" it is for a church to be open to all kinds of people, and how difficult it is for an old church to forsake its old ways. Therefore, the contrast between some old churches and some new churches is clearly seen when new churches choose to improvise their way into forms of church that break them away from restrictive old-church patterns.

The old adage "You can't teach an old dog new tricks" is too often true, short of the miraculous power of God, when it comes to assisting some parts of the church in learning to live out the gospel it proclaims. To a great degree, new churches have the opportunity—more difficult for older, "normal" churches to attain—to adopt the characteristics of a renewal movement. New churches sometimes stray far from the norms that have come to define the church. Old-line church people begin to ask aloud of these new churches:

> Is that church one of ours? Its members don't look like us. They don't act like us. What makes them think they are one of us? They don't put our denominational name or our denominational logo on their signs or their letterhead. The building they call their church doesn't look like a church. I hear their worship is more Pentecostal than Presbyterian. How are their visitors supposed to know from worship that one of these churches is one of ours? A friend tells me they marry interracial couples, they encourage children to receive holy communion, and they have a policy excluding the use of the American flag in the sanctuary. I am told that to become a member there, a person has to agree to tithe and to serve as a volunteer in the church or a community organization at least eight hours each month. How can one of our churches make such requirements of its members? It's just not normal!

Evolutionary Change

When significant change does occur in the church, it follows an evolutionary pathway. For me, the scientific theory of evolution describes the intricate process God used to put living things on earth. My admittedly simplistic understanding of the theory of evolution leads me to believe that a cornerstone of the process is the emergence of *mutant* forms of life—that is, *abnormal* forms—from within the ranks of an otherwise regular population of a species. Many of the emergent mutant forms of life never survive to pass along their aberrant traits. But when a portion of a species's population is isolated (i.e., *colonized*) from the whole for a long enough period of time—say as the result of continental drift, or from a cataclysmic earthquake—some of the mutations that occur within the isolated groups, particularly those that cause adaptations leading to the successful survival of the species, become the norm rather than the odd exception. In this case, two primary processes are largely responsible for changing a species in significant and positive ways, ensuring its survival and vitality: *mutation* and *isolation*.

Perhaps it is too farfetched to say that the effect of new churches formed in large numbers from the ranks of old-church populations of aging mainline denominations can be equated with the evolution of a living species of plant or animal. Yet the American Methodist experience seems sufficiently akin to this process to invite us to consider how it may be repeated in the church to bring renewal to the task of living the gospel.

Evolutionary Reform

It was out of the long-established, rigidly ordered, and thoroughly conventional Church of England that the Methodist movement emerged. Led by John Wesley; his prolific hymn-writing brother, Charles; and a small band of avid supporters in England, the American version of Methodism emerged late in the 18th century. Wesley never intended his efforts to lead to a new denomination. Yet from his work emerged the creation of one of the most influential Protestant bodies extant in the 19th and 20th centuries. Other old mainline denominations can offer similar accounts of their origins.

John Wesley was an ordained priest of the Church of England. Wesley's heart was for the common people, especially the poor, who were often isolated and excluded from the church by the circumstances of their lives and by the conduct of the church of his day. Wesley perceived that the established church inadequately provided for the spiritual welfare of England's people. Going outside the physical confines of the church, Wesley took the gospel to the people where they lived and worked. His preaching was spirited and evangelical in tone. Short of enough willing clergy, Wesley turned to lay leadership to preach and to conduct Methodist Societies, which were small groups devised for Bible study and the spiritual nurture of their participants. Wesley's notion of church led him to believe and teach that a right spiritual relationship with God should lead to social involvement to alleviate the pangs of suffering felt by the least of society's members, especially the poor and the oppressed.

Wesley and his followers won no favor with the established Anglican authorities. Theirs was a *mutant* form of church found unacceptable to the established church. They were persecuted in many ways. For example, clergy stirred up their Anglican laity, who in turn mobbed and destroyed Methodist chapels. More and more, the Methodists were isolated from the "mainline" of their day.

The Methodist form of church was particularly well suited to the frontier American setting. Once planted in America by early missionary evangelists such as Francis Asbury and Thomas Coke and by spirited black preachers such as Harry Hosier, the Methodist movement expanded rapidly. From 14,000 members in 1780, American Methodism grew to 1.5 million members by 1850. Both mutation of the forms of being church recognized in 18th-century England and *isolation* from the parent church—first in England, and more distantly in America—provided the evolutionary field for change in the way the Methodist Church understood its mission and lived out its calling to be the people of Christ. Though born of the Anglican tradition, the movement quickly took on a new shape. It increasingly distinguished itself from its parent and became more effective in conveying the good news of Christ to a spiritually hungry world.

Today, it is fair to say that the Methodist Church (now represented primarily by the United Methodist denomination) and other old mainline denominations are as mired in routine and resistant to change as was the English church of two and a half centuries ago. So the struggle for churches to remain faithful and vital communities of faith is an ongoing challenge in every era.

Freed from Christendom's Hold

Mainline stagnation and decline have not gone unnoticed. Today the aisles of religious bookstores are crowded with diagnostic reports decrying the spreading malaise within the mainline. Increasingly, church leaders recognize the gravity of the situation. Many say that something must be done about the church's precipitous losses in size and influence. Unfortunately, many of the people who have heard the wake-up call and who have proclaimed the need for renewal of the church, seem to think that the goal is to recover the old church of Christendom as it was at the height of its glory.

In his book *The Once and Future Church*, Alban Institute founder Loren Mead distinguishes between what he calls the Apostolic and Christendom paradigms of the church.[11] For about three centuries, the church, living out of the Apostolic paradigm, experienced a hostile world. At the heart of the church was the congregation. Being a Christian or identifying yourself with Christians could be a difficult, if not dangerous behavior. The church's values were the values of Jesus, learned from those who had known him, from his words as they were passed down from witness to hearer, and from scripture as it was being written. It was the church's commitment to these values that both distinguished it from the world and helped to sustain it as a community of God's people. Each member of the Christian community had a responsibility to carry the good news of the gospel into a hostile world. The congregation played a vital role in strengthening its beleaguered members. The boundary between the church and the world was clear. Joining the Christian community was not easy. Only those who held to the values of Jesus as they were known and expressed by the community were accepted into the fellowship of the church. Baptism was a powerful act symbolizing the distinctiveness of a life lived in the way of Christ. One can imagine that a person called by the name "Christian" had a sense that she was living in a world of which she was no longer a part.

Constantine and Christendom

The Roman Emperor Constantine's conversion to Christianity in the fourth century (313 A.D.) began a process that led to the erasure of much that had earlier distinguished the church from the world. In time, the church and the empire became largely indistinguishable. Consequently, the hostility of the world toward the church, vociferously expressed in the Apostolic age, was extinguished. Church membership and good citizenship were essentially indistinguishable. Sacred and secular were intricately bound. Within the Christendom paradigm of the church, it was no longer the primary role of the individual Christian to be a witness to the faith; it was increasingly the task of the empire to enlarge its realm of influence, because to do so meant that the church would be spread farther as well. The boundary between the church and the world was not where it had been in the Apostolic era. In the Christendom-era church, the boundary was located on the frontier between the empire and the rest of the world which the empire had not yet penetrated.

For most of the history of Christianity, Christendom has influenced the church. In some ways, it has served the church well. It has allowed the church's influence to grow, spreading its message throughout the world. It is a sensible way to live, when you think about it— the church supports its host government and culture and, in turn, the government and culture support the church. Even in the United

States, where a separation of church and state is constitutionally required, breaches in the church-state boundary are not uncommon.

When I was a boy, my hometown maintained so-called blue laws that forbade most businesses from operating on Sundays. Only the most necessary services—the pharmacist was able to fill drug prescriptions for a couple of hours after church—were allowed. Sunday was the church's day, and the law of the land worked to limit activities that would compete with the church. Such acts of support for the church have been rewarded by an almost universal loyalty of the church and its members to the nation and its leaders. For some, an absence of expressed patriotism is clear evidence of a lack of faith. Belief in God and country are signs of good citizenship and good Christianity.

Worshiping America

Following the terrorist attacks in New York and Washington on September 11, 2001, flags sprouted ubiquitously throughout the United States. Understandably, the nation's citizens wanted to show the world, and especially those who seek to destroy us, our strength and our loyalty to our democratic purposes as a country. I'm not a big flag-waver myself, but I mounted a bracket by my door and pulled out a long-folded flag from storage and let it wave for several weeks.

A pastor friend of mine serves a church that has never displayed an American flag in its sanctuary. To my knowledge, this congregation has never debated whether to have a U.S. flag in the church. But on the Sunday after September 11, members of a Sunday school class put a standing flag in place in the chancel without the knowledge of the pastor. When the flag was brought to his attention, he asked that it be removed. I would judge my friend to be socially liberal, but theologically orthodox and even conservative. In response to the plane attacks, he had chosen, like many other pastors, to hold a midweek prayer service. In his sermon, he relied heavily on the words of Dr. Martin Luther King, Jr. The pastor challenged members to draw upon their most deeply held Christian values when thinking of the horrors caused by the perpetrators of the attacks. The service included great hymns of the church, but no patriotic songs were sung. Likewise, none were included in services the next Sunday—the day the flag was introduced into the sanctuary. Believing his responsibility was to bring the word of God, and not the word of country, to the congregation, this pastor shaped his services in the weeks that followed accordingly. Perhaps predictably, he endured some scorching charges of disloyalty to country and was called unpatriotic. His challenge to Christendom's norms and the congregation's challenging response to his measured decision to exclude the national flag from the sanctuary and patriotic songs from worship, revealed that this old paradigm remains deeply rooted in the church today.

In contrast, the pastor of a local independent, nondenominational church displayed on the wall behind the pulpit a flag of enormous dimensions as the centerpiece of its worship center. I would guess that "The Battle Hymn of the Republic" was played and sung more than once in this church in the months after September 11. Hanging anything other than a cross or a flag in this church's worship space would, I think, be considered an abominable, if not idolatrous act. Yet, for churches like this one, the flag and cross serve equally as symbols of the church in the world today. This is only part of Christendom's lingering legacy.

Lost Favor

Like it or not, the ways of Christendom, and the protections and favoritism afforded the church for its loyalty and support of the nation, have eroded. Vestiges of Christendom remain, but the breakdown of the relationship between the church and the world is evident. Blue laws are a thing of the past. Zoning laws often prohibit church construction in neighborhoods where the church once was welcome. Merchant discounts, once a mainstay of commerce between retailers and churches, are a rarity. Clergy, as a group, are increasingly targeted for tax audits by the IRS. Landlords often refuse to lease space in business centers to new churches, fearing that other tenants will complain. Developers turn down generous offers to buy property for church construction in their planned developments.

Meanwhile, some parts of the church are intentionally stripping themselves of their own sacred identity, creating "seeker-friendly" worship spaces bereft of crosses, candles, stained glass, baptistries, pulpits, communion tables, or anything formerly connoting "church" to the culture. Some say this approach is the church's response to an overwhelmingly secularized society, as it attempts to draw unchurched people into the life of faith. On the other hand, is this kind of church conceding that society no longer values the distinctiveness of the church as much as it values American secular culture?

Whether the remnant Christendom-era church today lives in the false comfort of thinking that its security is in both Christ and the nation, or in the belief that it must become more secular to become more relevant, we are left with a tepid, if not innocuous church whose influence may be self-evident to its most loyal members, but is hardly noticed at all by the world. We are left with a church in need of a theology—a theology that distinguishes the church once again from the world and all that denies the values of Christ.

Christendom Era at an End

Christendom's role has fractured, according to Mead, and the church can depend on it less and less for its identity and its strength as an institution. In the American context, no other segment of the church has benefited more from Christendom than the mainline denominations. For this reason, many leaders of these churches decry the loss of Christendom. Many work as if it still exists; others dream of its recurrence. For many leaders in the mainline, the only church they have known and the only one they know how to lead is the church formed by the church's Christendom-shaped values. This state of affairs makes it inherently difficult for old churches, old denominations, and old-generation, old-style leaders to see any other way to be the church.

Rather than bemoan the loss of the relative comfort and certitude of Christendom, the church should hail the opportunity its breakdown provides for it to find itself again. This loosening of Christendom's grip on the church makes room for something to occur like the improvisational break in jazz, with all its risks and opportunities. Albert Murray says, "The break [in jazz] is an extremely important device both from the structural point of view and from its implications. It is precisely this disjuncture which is the moment of truth. . . . The moment of greatest jeopardy is your moment of greatest opportunity."[12] Although what a band plays after the break resembles what was played before it, the remainder of the performance is influenced and shaped by the direction taken in the break. Some of the past is shed, while some of the past is carried forward—preferably those parts beneficial to the success of the piece. Likewise, a church whose course is diverted from the mainstream direction it has long traveled can be systemically changed without altogether relinquishing all of its past qualities, practices, and features.

Hebrews' Predicament—and Ours

The substance of Christendom is so ingrained in the American church experience today that it is difficult for churches and their leaders who are acculturated to its way to be freed from its hold. This is no new predicament for communities of faith, as we see in the story told in the book of Numbers.

The Hebrew people have been brought away from Egypt through 40 years in the wilderness to the very cusp of the promised land of Canaan. At God's command, Moses selects men as spies from every tribe of Israel to go ahead of them to see this land. Moses says to them:

> Go up there into the Negeb, and go up into the hill country, and see what the land is like, and whether the people who live in it are strong or weak, whether they are few or many, and whether the land they live in is good or bad, and whether the towns that they live in are unwalled or fortified, and whether there are trees in it or not. Be bold, and bring some of the fruit of the land. (Numbers 13:17-20)

So the men go as Moses commanded and enter the promised land. At the Wadi Eshcol they cut down a branch bearing grapes so large that two men are needed to carry it suspended from a pole.

Upon returning to Moses and Aaron and the waiting congregation of Israelites, the spies show the people the fruit they have found. They describe the place they have seen as a land flowing with milk and honey and full of fruit, promising it to be a true respite from the poor land and bland fare encountered along the way of their wilderness journey. Yet, they say—and this is a big "yet"—"the people who live in the land are strong, and the towns are fortified and very large" (Num. 13:28). In a word, they are saying that the dangers of this new land far outweigh the benefits. Let's not go.

Caleb, one of the spies sent to Canaan by Moses, says without fear that they should at once go into the land and seize it. His is a minority opinion, though, for the others who go up with him again ring the bell of caution, saying that they are not strong enough to go up against the people they have seen in the land. The land itself, they say, devours people; and all of the people in it are giants! To these giants, they submit, "we seemed like grasshoppers."

The sense of fear of the unknown, driven by the hyperbole of the fearful spies, must have been palpable among the people gathered to hear their report. "Would that we had died in the land of Egypt! Or would that we had died in this wilderness," they complain (Num. 14:2). They question why God would have brought them all this way just to lose their lives and all that they love. "Would it not be better to go back to Egypt?" (Num. 14:3).

Disconcerting fears springing from the uncertainties of an unknown future can make even the severe bondage of the past and the tedium of wandering in a scarce wasteland seem a better path. But this story is not just about fear of what lies ahead when entering a new place, but also about leaving behind those things familiar to you that have given your life meaning. If all you have eaten for 40 years is manna, manna may seem to be what food is all about.

A Choice to Make

In many ways, the story from Numbers seems to be about the mainline church today. Christendom, its mainstay, has broken down. The journey is almost done. God is leading the church to a new environment—to a world thoroughly secularized and increasingly distinct from the church and the values of Jesus. Glimpses of what the future church may be are disconcerting to some in the mainline. Congregations or movements within mainline denominations that live out a jazzlike "break" through experimentation and improvisation on age-old themes like worship and liturgy and Christian education and theological interpretation are thought to be renegades who are trying to "take over the church." Much of the mainline resists going where these people want the church to go. Questions arise: "If we go where they want us to go [as the church], how will we know that we are still Presbyterians [or Lutherans, or Episcopalians, or Methodists]?" This fear-response pattern can be seen in microcosm in church leaders and in local congregations, and in macrocosmic ways in middle judicatories and in whole denominational bodies. And, as mainliners, we are increasingly aware of this experience and its incumbent tensions today.

I want to propose again, however, that the powerful pull of our customary and beloved practices of being the church of Christendom makes it difficult to let go of tired habits. In 40 years of wilderness-wandering, a lot of good and bad customs are acquired. In a few hundred years (a reasonable estimate of the age of many of the mainline denominations today) and in nearly 17 centuries under Christendom's influence, the church's habits and traditions are legion. Bondage to the routines of the past suppresses the church's capacity to take risks—a daring inherent to entering a new and unknown place. This reluctance to risk has the effect of snuffing out the Holy Spirit when God is ready to lead the church into new fields of mission. This timidity leaves the church being less than it can be, short of what it needs to be as the community of Christ's people.

In a jazz composition, this juncture between the traditions of the past and the unknowns of the future has been called a "bifurcation." Alluding to the contributions to jazz of saxophonist Ornette Coleman, writer and broadcaster Alyn Shipton says:

> When a musician comes along who is so revolutionary as to question everything that has happened to jazz, and who turns it on its head without losing touch with its traditions, then the development of the music reaches another of what Michel Serres, the French philosopher of science, calls "bifurcations"—forks in the road. It is not always clear which direction will turn out to be the main highway in the future, and sometimes even a brightly lit, well-directed route will suddenly peter out into little more than a dusty footpath.[13]

The Road Not Taken

It seems to me that the mainline church today stands at one of these bifurcations in its history. The route it takes will mean everything to the role it plays in the world. Any new path will be filled with uncertainties, but following a new path may be the only way for the church to succeed. Increasingly, I am convinced that most aging mainline churches are so bound to the familiar and comfortable (if not always beneficial) ways of their past that it will be difficult for them to step onto a new path to see where God will lead. I suspect that they *can* follow a new way, but many will do so only when others more courageous first go ahead, find the new future, and lead them there by the hand.

I believe that the best hope for such an outcome is the creation of large numbers of new churches by mainline denominations. New churches, if led by leaders unfettered by the constraints of the negative aspects of Christendom's hold on the church, and if allowed to improvise their approach to interpreting the faith to today's world, can go ahead of us like the spies sent into Canaan.

Some will return with warnings of what lies ahead, encouraging the church to stay put or to do its best to recover its past. But I am truly convinced that some of these new churches will show others a new way, and that the old churches will follow them and will become renewed and will serve God well. For this reason, I think new churches are our best hope for recovering our ability as mainliners to be the church we need to be.

The Exciting Adventure

In *Resident Aliens*, Hauerwas and Willimon state that "The decline of the old, Constantinian synthesis between the church and the world means that we American Christians are at last free to be faithful in a way that makes being a Christian today an exciting adventure."[14] Though, as Hauerwas and Willimon propose, American Christians are free to engage in an "exciting adventure" of faithfulness, many churches choose to remain bound to their old practices. Experimentation is rare. New ideas are quickly put down. Leaders who introduce too much change are ostracized and they become *weary in well doing* (Gal. 6:9 KJV).

Feeling the Call

My phone rang, and the pastor who called asked, "Steve, how can I be assigned to start a new church?" I knew him well enough to know that he was a strong leader and a hard worker. Having led a number of churches during his career, he was, by all accounts, a successful pastor. I was surprised at his interest in starting a new church. "Steve," he said, "I am tired of trying to get church people to see that there are other ways to be the church. There is so much the church can do, but everything new I propose is blocked by people who think the only good way to be the church is the old way—the way it was done half a century ago. I think I can start a church from scratch and have a better chance of leading a congregation that is faithful to what God wants it to be today."

Another pastor, coming to my office fresh from seminary, said he believed he had the gifts required to reach young adults who have had very little, if any, involvement with the church. He had a dream of starting a new church that could do, in his opinion, what no existing church could free itself to do. He was given the opportunity to pursue his dream, and a new church was born. Its defined mission was to introduce generation Xers (born 1961–1981) and young adults with families to the gospel of Jesus Christ. When friends have asked about visiting this church, I have cautioned them to be prepared for a unique experience. Worship is fast-paced, filled with drama, illuminated by projected visual images, and saturated by loud music. *Really* loud.

On its inaugural worship Sunday, this congregation gathered up several hundred people from the surrounding community. During worship, I noticed an energetic young man in the church's praise band, playing a pulsating electric guitar. He appeared to be having a great time. After the service, I introduced myself. My personal and professional curiosity led me to ask him how long he had known the church's founding pastor. I knew that the pastor was a musician who had lived in the town for some time as an adolescent. "Oh," said the guitarist, "I just met him. He kept coming into the music store where I work, buying equipment and supplies for this new church. One day he asked me if I wanted to play in his new praise band, and here I am. Man, this is the first time I've been in church in 10 years . . . and I'm hooked!" Six months later, I again visited this newborn church, and there he was, pounding away at the strings of his instrument, looking very comfortable with his newfound spiritual family.

This case illustrates what I think Willimon means when he writes, "What we once knew theologically, we now know experientially: Tertullian was right—Christians are not naturally born . . . Christians are intentionally made by an adventuresome church, which has again learned to ask the right questions to which Christ alone supplies the right answers."[15]

An Alien Island in the Culture

New churches are like fresh canvases upon which colorful paintings of the church are created. A new church can break away from some of the forms and constraints long imposed on the church by Christendom's influential force and by the routines of its own past. Every new person joining the adventurous journey called the church is like a brush stroke added to the painting. This kind of church, with its enthusiastic congregants, can distinguish itself from its environment in the world, and from a tired, worn-out church that has become comfortable with itself and with the world. This "colony" of Christians, as it is described by Hauerwas and Willimon, is like an "island of one culture in the middle of another."[16] Christians are invited to become an "alien" people, distinguished by their choice to live like Christ in a community of other faithful believers. This church is not isolationist in the sense that it withdraws itself from contact with the world. In fact, the alien colony of Christ's people needs to be seen by the world so that its values can be known. According to Hauerwas and Willimon, "Nowhere in the Sermon [on the Mount] are believers encouraged to abandon this life or the world. Rather, we are to see the world aright, to grab hold of the world wisely. The world is a place of trial and testing for disciples, but also a place of great opportunity for serving the 'least of these' and thereby serving Christ."[17]

Often today, the church—and I am speaking essentially of the mainline church, which I know best—has become more of a franchising religious institution made up of its franchisee churches than a connection of related, distinctively Christian communities whose primary task is to show what God is like to the world. I, for one, am not interested in starting new churches simply to help my denomination to become the number-one retailer of religion in the country. To critics who say, "We have enough churches, and we don't need to start any more," I have to say that I agree. We do not need more churches if the ones we create are just like the churches we already have, and if they attract members who will simply perpetuate the bad habits of a church that has lost its vision for being a living people of God. But—and I am thoroughly convinced of this—we do need many more churches whose members choose to live in ways that seem peculiar to the world. We need churches whose members take seriously the teachings and example of Jesus. We need churches that choose not to be accommodating to the world when the world's ways contradict the way of Jesus. I believe we have a better chance now of creating this kind of church when new churches are formed than by trying to renew old churches whose resistance to change is strong.

Innovations from the Margins

Futurist Joel Barker observes that major paradigm shifts in an organization's or institution's way of doing business are often generated by people located around the margins of the organization rather than by those who are clearly insiders.[18] This observation may explain why so much of the experimentation being introduced in the church today in worship and music—for example, so-called contemporary worship; seeker-sensitive services; praise bands and choruses; and video projection—has first been introduced by independent churches, or by churches whose parent body is young enough that it retains the movement quality long ago lost by most mainline bodies.

It does the church of Christ no good if experimentation (improvisation) leads only to the addition of catchy, quirky, or seductive worship aimed at capturing a better market share of the religious set in a particular community. I often tell church leaders, "If you want your church to grow in membership, I can tell you how to make it grow. That's a marketing question. But I would prefer to talk to you about how to make your church grow toward becoming a distinctive community of faith—that's a theological question." If the issue is war or terrorism or the death penalty or genetic manipulation or abortion or the environment or racism or whatever, I want the world to be able to look at the church to see a community whose members have already looked to Jesus and to the teachings of scripture, who have deliberately set about discerning how to respond to these issues, and who live out of an ethic that distinguishes itself as Christian. Certainly, I don't mean that there is always only one way the church can understand what God's way is when faced with a perplexing ethical dilemma. But the church should be able to exercise its best judgment based upon what it knows best, Jesus and his way, and not upon what the world wants to hear, the most popular point of view, the safest and most acceptable solution, or the choice that puts the church in the world's favor.

Improvising by the Rules

It is important to understand this point about improvisation: When a jazz musician improvises, as when he is playing the break, it may seem that he takes off altogether on his own, playing notes randomly without paying attention to what's going on with the rest of the band. He may seem to be going against everything else the band's players want to do with the piece. The band may seem to be at the mercy of the soloist, just hoping that they can keep up and that he will come back to a point where they can all play together again. Even to allow a single musician to go off on his own in the middle of a piece seems counterintuitive. Sticking to a written score would be more sensible, right? Playing together in harmony—that's the way to make music people like listening to, right?

But the soloist playing the break is playing a much more predictable role than it might appear. He is playing music, after all, and certain rules have to be followed. A thread of these rules runs through every measure and every bar played, while all around the rules the skilled improviser runs around, over and under, inside and outside the rules, testing and teasing to see how far he can stray without leaving behind everyone and everything that holds him to the piece. It is this kind of *exciting adventure* that will enliven and shape the church whose members are more keenly interested in being faithful than in accommodating traditions that have long since lost their meaning.

Beyond Christendom

On November 18, 2001, I was up at 4 A.M. standing in inky darkness on top of a mountain in the Appalachians. Looking up, I could see an astonishing array of stars and planets. A sliver of moon had earlier disappeared below the horizon, making the darkness especially dark around the stars' brilliant little points of light. Living in a city, as I do, I seldom witness this kind of sky view. It was extraordinary. The position and movement of the stars and the constellations formed by them were predictable. The North Star held firm to its place; Orion hunted his way across the sky; the Big Dipper contained its fill of the heavens.

A Light Show of Meteors

But this seemingly fixed and stable vision of the sky was broken, first by one, then by a dozen, and soon by scores of meteoric displays of light swishing across my view. This event was what had prompted me to set my alarm so that I could get up and stand in the cold November air. It was the Leonid meteor shower, and it lived up to its billing as a great light show. Sometimes I saw a mere point of light travel with great speed a very short distance across my field of view. Then, I saw another, coming from another direction, streaking by with a long tapering tail. Then, two at a time, or three, each one seeming to travel along its own pathway from one edge of my view to the other.

The predictability of the night sky seemed disrupted by the meteors' random fly-bys. In truth, the meteors, though out of sync with the usual night sky, were following their own predictable routes through space. After all, I knew to be awake on a particular night at a particular time because someone smarter than I knew that the meteors would appear. Of course, no one could predict each one's precise path, or the specific frequency of appearance, or whether a tail would appear on one and not on another. But what seemed random and out of sync to me was, in fact, part of a grander scheme made up of multiple astral phenomena that happened at the same time within my range of view.

Like meteors, new churches, *if* they are a new kind of post-Christendom church, can coexist with old-paradigm churches, but they will forever change our conceptions of what God's church can be. These on-the-frontier churches, now or two centuries from now, can help the church find its way into the human environment of the day so that the world can see God disclosed and at work.

A Church Like Salt

Jesus says his followers are the salt of the earth (Matt. 5:13). Salt has amazing qualities. It can preserve food or wood by protecting them from decay; it can enhance the flavor of food. Salt has a less familiar, but more dynamic, use as a flux in making stoneware pottery. A flux acts as a catalyst to lower the melting point of glaze-making glass found naturally imbedded in rich stoneware clays. Salt-glazed stoneware relies entirely upon salt for its glazed surface. A potter heats her unglazed wares in a kiln to a cherry-red temperature of about 2300 degrees Fahrenheit. When the kiln reaches and sustains this temperature, pounds of common table salt are introduced into the kiln through ports in its side and arched roof. Immediately, the salt vaporizes upon contact with the atmosphere of the heated kiln's interior. It is then that the salt's amazing magic goes to work. Acting as a flux, the sodium vapor released from the heated salt coats every surface of the pottery stacked in the kiln, causing the naturally occurring glass (silica) found in the clay to melt out onto the surface to form a smooth cloak of glaze. It is one of the most durable ceramic surfaces made. Although the salt does not become the glaze, it is required if the glaze is to appear.

Like salt cast into the heat of a kiln, the post-Christendom church, while trying to be a "living, breathing, witnessing colony of truth,"[19] can draw new life out of old-paradigm churches. For this alchemy to work, mainline leadership, strategies, policies, and resources must allow new churches the freedom to investigate new pathways of faithful ministry, ensuring that new churches have the chance to become authentic communities of faith and not merely franchises of a tired mainline.

Chapter Four

Mainstreaming the Mainline

[G]lasnost *(new thinking) must always precede* perestroika *(restructuring).*
—C. Kirk Hadaway and David A. Roozen

People who dig in their heels and try to cling to yesterday's good ideas are roadblocks to progress.
—Michael Dell

You have a name of being alive, but you are dead. Wake up, and strengthen what remains and is on the point of death.
—Revelation 3:1b-2a

THE YEAR 2002 SAW A PRECIPITOUS decline in the value of many once prominent high-technology and dot-com companies. Having most of my pension account invested in domestic stocks made me a bit smug when my earnings far exceeded those realized by colleagues who took a more cautious, conservative approach. My smugness soon turned to humility when most stock values took a nosedive. I found some consolation in knowing that I was in the good company of others who had followed the same course. Just as quickly, as some tech companies rose to prominence, many succumbed to the quirks of the U.S. and world economies. Yet a few weathered the storm and continued to flourish in an unsettled economy.

Flexibility and Speed

As I write this chapter, evidence of this capacity for survival by such companies is as close as my fingertips. In front of me is a desktop computer. To my left is a laptop plugged into a port replicator. Dell, the source of all this hardware, also hosts two Web sites for me.

According to Helen Bond, writing for *American Way* magazine. Dell Computer Corporation's founder, Michael Dell, started his now $36-billion megabusiness from his college dorm room in 1984 with $1,000 and a good idea.[1] Dell's legendary success is based on its build-to-order PC purchasing process:

• Go online.
• Tell Dell what you want your computer to do.
• Dell designs a custom PC to suit your needs and sends you a proposal and the cost.
• If you like the product and the price, you order and pay online.
• In a few days, your computer is delivered to your door.

(I'm easily impressed by innovation, but I was totally blown away when the hard drive failed on my first Dell laptop, and Dell sent a service agent to my office within 24 hours to replace the hard drive at no cost to me. Try getting service like that from your cable TV provider!)

Dell's success is largely explained by two words: *flexibility* and *speed*. Michael Dell describes his firm's corporate culture this way: "Our culture is agile, results-oriented, it sets aggressive goals for itself, it's challenging, it's internally very self-critical. We don't spend a lot of time congratulating ourselves for things that have happened. We spend most of our time thinking about what we are going to do in the future to improve things and make them better. We continue to set higher and higher standards."[2]

Church as Countercultural

Although for companies like Dell, change is normal, it may be anathema[3] to the church. Says Michael Dell: "If you change something at Dell, people say, 'Oh great, that's good, something has changed.' If you don't change things at Dell, people say, 'Why don't you change it? What's the problem, there must be a problem.'"⁴ By contrast, the response to change in the church is more often, "Why did you change that? That's not our way of doing it."

A key to Dell's success in expanding its reach around the world is its ability to remain clear about what it is trying to accomplish— without those few people in the center of the organization supposing that they know the only way to reach the market in far-flung places. "Basically," says Dell, "what you have to do is have a clear strategy, a framework for decisions, and almost a philosophy for ideas and strategies that can permeate many different kinds of businesses around the company."⁵ The mainline church can learn from Dell's model. No one would suggest that the mainline church needs to abandon its *first cause* (that is, pursuing what it means to "love the Lord your God with all your heart, and with all your soul, and with all your mind . . . [and] love your neighbor as yourself" [Matt. 22:37-39]). Like all of the people of God, we mainliners are always called to be, in the language of Willimon and Hauerwas, a "countercultural phenomenon, a new *polis*, called church."⁶ If the *center* of the mainline church (that is, its leaders, its organizations and institutions, its doctrines, its strategies) can constantly clarify and communicate the church's *first cause*, holding its constituents accountable to it, then it should be able to let the church at the local level define its own way to present Christ and to create the community called church. This indigenous approach to church formation should not in any way threaten loss of the church's core values for which the Protestant mainline stands. The church leaders should allow the church, in its most local and intimate manifestation, to take on myriad forms appropriate to the time and place. Jackson W. Carroll calls these innovations "local ecclesiologies," noting that they are "organizational forms and practices through which local congregations attempt to give expression to the gospel and received ecclesial traditions in ways appropriate to their local social and cultural contexts."⁷

If the mainline is to survive as a vehicle for carrying the gospel to the world, it will have to have local churches whose ministries can quickly adapt to local community change. This is not to say that churches have to follow trends or fads. Drop-down screens in our sanctuaries, cappuccino in the narthex, and worship hallmarked by "praise choruses"—these things are not panaceas for what ails the church, although they may be quite appropriate when the church tries to relate the gospel to contemporary culture. A church whose community was once entirely English-speaking but whose neighborhood population is now multilingual, will want to offer its ministries in more than one language. It may mean that a church whose founding members were once the civic and business leaders of the community will have to learn how to engage its new working-class neighbors in church life. It may mean that the once-weekly Sunday worship service at 11 A.M. is complemented by services conducted throughout the week to accommodate the schedules of people who work on Sunday. And shortly after adapting to one change, a church may have to change its ways again, since our U.S. culture and our communities are constantly changing.

When Change Becomes the Norm

I was reared in a community where racial diversity was close to nonexistent. Until my senior year of high school, I attended racially segregated schools. Jim Crow laws ensured that I could sit downstairs in movie theaters while black teenagers sat only in the balcony, and twin water fountains were distinguished by signs reading COLORED ONLY and WHITE ONLY. Restaurants and restrooms in my town were for black or white people, never for both races. Today, these outward manifestations of racism have been eradicated, and American society is as racially integrated as it has ever been in the nation's history—an indication that significant change has occurred.

In my boyhood, a nearby town had a small Roman Catholic church, but I don't recall ever knowing a Catholic until I was an adult. Jews, Muslims, Hindus, Buddhists, and Sikhs were not even part of my religious vocabulary. Today I live in a neighborhood whose residents represent all these religions and more. American culture increasingly shows its capacity to change.

In my youth, our suburban neighborhood was occupied by working-class, home-owning, white, mostly churchgoing young adults whose homes and cars were always unlocked and whose homes were safe havens for any kid who needed a drink of water or just a place to get away from Mom and Dad. Today, in my boyhood neighborhood one increasingly witnesses the presence of senior adults, renters, people of numerous races and religious backgrounds, the sound of people speaking Spanish, and waves of Hispanic music wafting from rolled-down car windows at a nearby community center. The neighborhood is also increasingly a place of locked doors. The streets and houses are the same as they were more than four decades ago, but the community makeup has changed considerably.

My family moved to this neighborhood in 1954, and my parents became charter members of a new Methodist church a year earlier. As I noted earlier, my parents had both Presbyterian and Primitive Baptist religious backgrounds, but were uninvolved in church in the early years of their marriage. If a new church were started today in the same location, its membership, worship style, and ministry programs might be starkly different from what they were five decades ago. Despite the changes in the church's community, and its merger with another congregation in the early 1970s, the makeup of its mission and membership remains largely unchanged today. Despite significant community transition, the church my family helped create has done little to adapt to the changes evident in its vicinity.

In the mainline today, churches like my boyhood congregation are not numbered in the dozens or even hundreds, but in the thousands. Honestly, many of them remain unchanged from their past ways because they were initially successful and their ministries were satisfactory for years. But if we are to take a cue from Michael Dell's approach to business, we need churches whose mission is informed by a commitment to the *first cause* of the church. The church can be the distinctive people of God in the world, whose leaders and members speedily adapt its local forms of ministry to the indigenous requirements of the community's people.

Change and Order Go Together

Church consultant Bill Easum writes, "The emerging world is being defined by speed, blur, and flux. In such a world, the future belongs to those who can change the fastest and easiest, with the least amount of personal conflict, without losing their spiritual equilibrium."[8] This approach does not change the fundamental core values of the church; it does call for an attitude whereby change is the norm, not a dreaded exception in the life of a church. An inflexible church would elicit the comment of an astute observer, "Nothing has changed. What's the problem? There must be a problem."

If you listen to jazz, you know that it is the constant introduction of change (improvisation) that makes jazz interesting and rich with texture and color and life. In fact, it's not truly jazz, I suppose, without improvisation. You also recognize that an underlying order always supports even the most heavily improvised piece. *Change* and *order* go hand in hand. In the 1930s swing era of jazz, a movement led by some forward-looking musicians was known as *mainstreaming* (distinct in meaning from today's notion of putting people with special needs into regular living, work, and educational settings). Mainstreaming encouraged solo improvisation on musical scores without relinquishing the connection to the known chord sequences for that song or instrumental piece.

Although an improvised solo may appear to compete with a composition, in fact it is complementary to it, enriching the entire piece and eliciting the best of its potential. I believe that mainline denominations can find their future in this *mainstreaming* image. We major in doing church in the way of well-practiced chord sequences we have learned and repeated for a century or two. It is not necessary to abandon all that the church has become. But we do not do so well at encouraging solo improvisation by our churches. In an aging mainline body, encouragement is rarely given to avant-garde churches. We prefer predictability over apparent randomness when it comes to church behavior. But the Babel-like chaos of an experimenting church need not be feared if we understand that it is sometimes from chaotic behavior that we see new sacred experience emerge. By encouraging improvisation by courageous churches whose members are willing to follow God's lead into new places of ministry, the whole of the mainline can likewise be enriched, empowered, and renewed. Here are three examples showing how apparently chaotic behavior leads to rich new ways of doing things.

Retelling the Message

First, Janna Tull Steed, author of *Duke Ellington: A Spiritual Biography*, says of jazz:

> It's not simply that musicians change a note here or there or that they add embellishments, or that they make up maybe a little new melody.

The ones who are true artists do something more than that. They recreate, they reform, they reshape, and they do that out of their own interiority, out of their own heart and soul and the history of their own lives. That is the process that is essential to both religious contemplation and to art.[9]

A similar process is essential to the vitality of our aging mainline denominations. We have in our histories, in our core Protestant values, in our rich spiritual heritages the resources we need. That's our interiority, to use Steed's word—to recreate, reform, and reshape ourselves; not to change the message, but to change how we communicate the message from time to time, from place to place.

Second, I have on my office wall an image taken by the Hubble telescope of one of the most fascinating structures ever viewed in the universe. It is the Eagle Nebula, found in the Serpens constellation. From a great distance, the nebula appears to be a chaotic mass of jumbled stars and clouds of gas. But a closer view reveals that within its topsy-turvy shape is a well-defined structure, including distinctive, towering fingers of gas and matter. An even closer look reveals that from within these structures, which are the component parts of the larger nebula, new stars, like our own sun, are being born. This is a jarring revelation to someone who thinks God finished creation long ago. Though the Genesis account notes that God created our solar system's sun on the fourth day, and it was done, it appears that God is, in fact, continuing to hatch an ever-changing universe full of new suns, and presumably planets and moons and all kinds of exotic astral structures.

Like this evolving universe, the church can and must be an incubator where new forms of Christian community are born. If we can learn to lead with the core values of the church from our denominational centers, while allowing, even encouraging, improvisation at the local-church level, we may find our future. It is this balance between control and chaos that gives us hope as a church.

Chaos and Control
Third, West African influence has been seen historically in the Deep South church dance tradition of ring-shouting. Dancers form a circle in the center of the floor, then shuffle in a counterclockwise direction with arms extended and shoulders hunched. Others outside the circle

join in with clapping and stomping, building up a pulsating rhythm. tion. In time, people begin to scream and spin, possessed by a form of religious hysteria. Despite this chaotic movement of bodies, everything is under control, with participants taking care that possessed brothers and sisters don't hurt themselves when they fall in writhing ecstasy. The point of the occasion is to "get religion" by becoming possessed—but in the correct way through this complicated and sacred ritual.[10] This is the point—that the church performs best when a fine balance exists between the poles of control and chaos.

Systemic vs. Programmatic Change

If a jazz saxophonist like John Coltrane could use his horn to evoke sacred strains from a cacophony of notes in his masterwork "A Love Supreme"; and if new stars can emerge out of a jumbled maelstrom of gas, dust, and radiation; and if complex ritual, characterized by ecstatic physical movement in West African sacred dancing, can provide for some a pathway to God, then perhaps a comparable system-jarring act like mainstreaming new churches into the mainline can lead to new forms of faithful Christian community as well.

If a mainstreaming of new churches into the mainline is to occur to the degree that is required to precipitate needed changes, it must have the support of the top levels of mainline leadership (for example, national and regional leaders such as bishops, presidents, executive presbyters, judicatory staff, program and agency heads, and key clergy and laity). If we still possessed the movement quality of our earlier histories as mainliners, we might expect that new churches would be spun off by strong, self-confident, mission-minded congregations, or they might erupt organically within pioneering new communities. But we have too few congregations ready today to take the lead in planting new churches in the numbers required to bring hope to our common denominational mission. If large numbers of new (and free to improvise) mainline churches are to be initiated, then denominational strategies and leaders will have to reflect a strong commitment to church extension ministry. This task calls for a more *systemic* than *programmatic* approach toward denominational renewal.

I use the word *programmatic* in the way we describe a series of coded instructions devised to control the operation of a computer.

This undesirable approach to the church's mission has too often been tried without success. Top-level judicatory leaders can challenge the church to stay the course of meeting the church's *first cause* mission; they can provide encouragement, logistical support, and resources. But we do not need the top echelon of leaders to tell congregations the only right, programmed way to do it. New (and old) worshiping communities need to be free to make discoveries on their own. This is a church's opportunity to play the *break* in a tune called "This Is the Church for Right Here, Right Now." This way, each new local church can shape its ministry so that it meets the indigenous needs of the people in its community. No single canned program and no set and unchanging mode for "church" will suffice to bring vitality to waning mainline denominations.

I use the word *systemic* to recall a horticultural analogy whereby nutrition is passed through the roots of the plant so it is imparted to all of the plant's tissues. This thorough, organic approach, ensures that the whole of the system is affected.

And Are We Yet Alive?
United Methodism has tried on many occasions over two decades to use the programmatic approach to bring renewed vitality to a seriously declining mainline body of churches.

The first warning of our impending demise that was taken seriously by denominational leaders may have come from Bishop Richard B. Wilke, of the Arkansas Area, in his 1986 book *And Are We Yet Alive?: The Future of The United Methodist Church* (Abingdon, 1986). The good bishop minced no words in describing the seriousness of the denomination's condition. He opened his first chapter with these words:

> Our sickness is more serious than we at first suspected. We are in trouble, you and I, and our United Methodist Church. We thought we were just drifting, like a sailboat on a dreamy day. Instead, we are wasting away like a leukemia victim when the blood transfusions no longer work.
>
> Once we were a Wesleyan revival, full of enthusiasm, fired by the Spirit, running the race set before us like a sprinter trying to win the prize. The world was our parish; we were determined to "publish the glad tidings in the full light of sun." Our Wesley-inspired dream and

directive was to "spread Scriptural holiness" across the continent. Circuit riders raced over hill and valley. New churches were established in every hamlet. Our missionaries encircled the globe. Now we are tired, listless, fueled only by the nostalgia of former days, walking with a droop, eyes on the ground, discouraged, putting one foot ahead of the other like a tired old man who remembers, but who can no longer perform.[11]

Although Bishop Wilke issued a clarion call for us to wake up, shape up, and get on with being the church, his prescription for renewal fell short. He suggested that we encourage longer pastoral appointments to local churches, cut the fat from our church structures, increase ministry to singles, revive the Wesleyan class system, and promote Bible study that is more meaningful and less academic (the seed of the highly successful Disciple Bible Study series).

Staying in Egypt

Following Wilke, two prominent lay members of the denomination, James W. Holsinger, Jr., and Evelyn Laycock made their own passionate call for sweeping changes in the organization and policies of United Methodism in *Awaken the Giant: 28 Prescriptions for Reviving the United Methodist Church*. Their ideas for renewal included the abolition of quotas based on race, ethnicity, age, gender, and "handicapping condition" as a basis for selecting UMC leaders; an end to the guaranteed appointment system for ordained ministers; election of a CEO for the denomination; and a requirement that all seminary students be trained in evangelism.[12]

In 1988, the United Methodist Council of Bishops initiated a quadrennial emphasis and theme for the denomination called *Vital Congregations—Faithful Disciples: Vision for the Church*. This effort, in fact, clearly voiced many relevant concerns facing the churches and the denomination. The bishops called for local churches to take up the task of ministering in the local communities to a rapidly changing and somewhat troubled world. They used the language of journey, and they talked about the imminent risks inherent in traveling to strange lands. They acknowledged that we would rather stay in Egypt than cross the wilderness.[13] Despite their impassioned call for change and response to the needs of people in our church's communities, they may have underestimated the inherent resistance to change in local churches and their leaders. As a pastor at the time, I never felt that I was given enough power and freedom to be very *improvisational* in leading my church. As an ordained elder, my appointment was guaranteed, but where I might be appointed was not! Programs and materials were created—*Growth Plus: The Vision* by Joe A. Harding (Discipleship Resources, 1987); *Vision 2000: Planning for Ministry into the Next Century* by Joe A. Harding and Ralph W. Mohney (Discipleship Resources, 1989); *Quest for Quality in the Church: A New Paradigm* by Ezra Earl Jones (Discipleship Resources, 1993). But the passage of more than a decade has demonstrated little change in growth or innovation that resulted from this emphasis. From January 1, 1987, through January 1, 2000, United Methodists experienced a loss in lay membership of 752,806 people within its jurisdictional conferences (primarily representing its membership within the United States), whereas the number of clergy members increased by 6,119.[14]

The Past as a Clue to the Future

The mainline has known a better way before. The history of the North Carolina Conference demonstrates how mainstreaming new congregations can bring about the renewal of declining denominations.

The first example comes from the period following the end of the Civil War to the beginning of World War I. Today, the North Carolina Conference has about 840 churches. Between 1870 and 1920, 579 new churches were established in eastern North Carolina. On average, this increase represents the creation, in a mostly rural region, of about 12 new churches every year for half a century. Though many of these churches today are small, have aging memberships, and are struggling for survival, for numerous generations many of these churches have been the lifeblood of Methodist ministry in their communities. Remarkably, most of these churches remain open today, despite community population losses, demographic shifts within their mission areas, and widespread resistance among congregational leaders to the kind of innovation and adaptation required to meet the indigenous needs of their community's current residents. This mammoth movement to begin new churches put Methodism in essentially every area served by a post office in eastern North Carolina. In

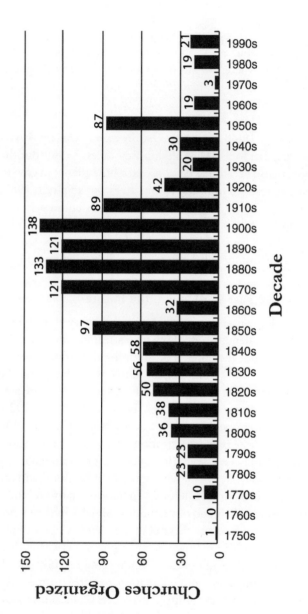

Figure 3: Churches Organized by Decades, 1750–2000
North Carolina Conference, UMC

fact, it has been said that there were, at one time, more Methodist churches than post offices! These Methodist outposts, with their educated clergy, played an important role in reaching out to an increasingly well-educated population whose adults wanted to ensure that their children would be well trained. Strong support given to free public education by the Methodists (by supporting public policies that ensured access for all to free public elementary and secondary schools) and an equally strong commitment to Sunday schools appealed to this emerging new class of people.

A Challenge to Start Churches

The second example comes from the period just after the conclusion of World War II. Early in the 1950s, Bishop Paul Neff Garber, presiding over the Richmond Area of the then Methodist Church, challenged the members of the North Carolina Conference (at the time, part of the Richmond Area) to begin 70 new churches in 70 months.

This was a time of dramatic demographic transition in eastern North Carolina. The successful end of World War II was followed by suburban growth around towns and cities. This trend was driven by the needs of migrating town-and-country workers seeking city jobs. This movement of large numbers of people from rural and small-town areas to suburban and city settings accelerated the decline of many churches outside the cities, while bolstering the growth of new and existing suburban and city churches.

Churches to Serve Population Shifts

Whereas previously most eastern North Carolina Methodist churches were in rural areas and most Methodists were members of these churches, this shift in population led to most Methodists joining suburban and city churches, while most churches remained in rural and small-town communities. Garber's intent to begin so many new churches was derived from his recognition that if we did not follow our mostly young-adult Methodists from their former homes to their new communities, we would lose them as denominational constituents, perhaps to other churches, and perhaps to no church at all. Garber was lauded as a champion by denominational leaders for his promotion of church-extension ministry. Although the goal of 70 churches in 70 months was not quite met, in the years between 1953 and 1993, 94 new churches were organized, most of them under Garber's leadership.

Of the 94 new churches started in the four decades between 1953 and 1993, 77 remained open in 1993. Among those remaining open and active were some churches with the largest membership and worship attendance in the conference area. The 77 newest churches open in 1993 represented about 9 percent of the total number of churches in the conference. Remarkably, these newest churches accounted for fully 65 percent of the net membership increase realized since 1953 for the entire conference. Simply stated, had the conference, under the visionary and progressive leadership of Bishop Garber and others who joined with him, not begun so many new churches at this time of great demographic movement from rural to suburban and urban settings, North Carolina surely would be among those conferences whose memberships have seen steep and debilitating declines. The conference has grown in membership more than 35 percent since 1950 and by nearly 8 percent since the merger in 1968 (with the Evangelical United Brethren) that created the United Methodist Church. The denomination as a whole has declined in membership by 18 percent since the merger.[15]

Chords and Riffs

I contend that each of these historic infusions of large numbers of new churches into the ranks of many older churches caused a systemic change in the outlook and commitment of the conference leadership, and consequently led to the mobilization of leadership and resources required to meet the goal. Conference leadership moved away from commiserating about the unfortunate decline of rural churches toward thinking that change *is* happening and that the church must address change as it occurs. This was an *improvisational mainstreaming* moment for this conference. The foundational *chord structures*, so to speak, didn't change, but a few bold leaders took the conference into a solo riff, which enlivened and enriched what would otherwise have become a lackluster tune for this conference through the '60s, '70s, '80s, and '90s.

A commitment to new-church development in the 1950s was not universally shared by all conference leaders. Conference records indicate that soon after the departure of Bishop Garber, the number of new-church "starts" plunged dramatically. But so long as starting new churches was held up as a conference core value, the effort continued and excelled. Some of the best and brightest young pastors were deployed to lead the new churches. Uncustomary methods (at least to Methodists at the time), such as tent revivals, were used to attract potential members.

A Board of Missions was incorporated for the purpose of raising funds to be loaned to new churches for building their first facilities. The conference approved loaning significant sums to this emerging loan agency, which in turn could be loaned out to new churches. Interest gained from these loans, after repaying conference advances, became the source for increasingly large amounts of money to be loaned for church extension. A builders club, a voluntary organization whose members agreed to pay $10 on three occasions each year—thus its name, the Ten Dollar Club—was formed, quickly recruiting more than 4,000 members to its ranks. District and city boards of mission and church extension were organized to support local new-church efforts. Prefabricated metal buildings, some of them similar to World War II Quonset huts, were used as first places of worship and were affectionately, if sometimes derisively, called "steel chapels." Other new churches started in storefront business sites, and one got its start in an abandoned barn.

From Quonset Hut to Big Steeple

From its original steel chapel building, White Plains Church grew to have more than 1,200 in worship in three services each week. The congregation was the second Methodist church in the then-small town of Cary, North Carolina. Since those times, the little town of about 7,000 has grown to a population exceeding 103,000. Today, four United Methodist churches serve the city, and a fifth is on the drawing board. White Plains Church has been the beneficiary of loans, grants, leadership, and other resources put in place during the Garber era of new-church development. In turn, it has aided in establishing other new churches nearby, including a Spanish-language congregation, and is a leader in mission outreach ministries. This is but one example of the best of what the mainline has accomplished in the past. Do we have the will and the way to do it again?

First Steps to Mainstream the Mainline

Let me paraphrase a statement I quoted earlier in this chapter by Dell Computer's Michael Dell. What if this were the attitude of the Protestant mainline today?

> Our *denomination* (*or church*) is agile, results-oriented; it sets aggressive goals for itself; it's challenging, it's internally very self-critical. We don't spend a lot of time congratulating ourselves for things that have happened. We spend most of our time thinking about what we are going to do in the future to improve things and make them better. We continue to set higher and higher standards.

Does this sound anything like the mainline today? If not, is it possible for our cumbersome, hardened, resistant judicatory structures to change? Can those who lead us now be the leaders to bring about the changes we need to make? Can we find within our spiritual *interiority* the freedom, will, courage, and hope to take the necessary steps required to bring new life to our aging denominations? I suspect we can, but it will not be a task for the faint of heart. *In fact, I am convinced that what is called for is the most dramatic reorientation of outlook, strategy, leadership, and resources ever undertaken by the mainline denominations.* I am equally certain that if the mainline does not change, and soon, its demise as a primary force for spreading the good news is inevitable. Like a once-bright star shining in the heavens, it will collapse into a merely warm cinder as a reminder of its once significant place in God's church.

So how do we begin to mainstream the mainline with new churches? I propose the following 10-point strategy as a way the mainline may begin the process of mainstreaming new-church development into its core.

Make New Churches the Priority

1. *Declare from the denominational center that new-church development is its priority task.* A mainline denomination's center consists of its top level of judicatory decision makers and policy agencies. Support for new-church development from its top leaders is essential. If these leaders are not for new-church development, their

energies either will be put in force against it, or directed toward other causes to the exclusion of new-church ministry.

Predictably, choosing new-church development as the priority task of a denomination will awaken those whose passions are engaged by other missions and causes. Setting this priority is not meant to disparage the many important missions sponsored by the mainline. But, the fact is, if we do not continue to create vital local-church ministries, the base of support for these other important ministries, which has sustained them for many decades, will be gone and they will be lost. We are beyond the point of choosing between the creation of new churches and other good missions of the church. In this case, the question of which came first, the chicken or the egg, can be answered. It is because we first had strong churches that the mainline was able to create and support other large-scale ministries. If we do not have strong local churches, the mainline will not be capable of carrying out other cooperatively supported missions and ministries. It is time now to declare that the mainline is facing an unparalleled crisis. This crisis will not be fixed by doing more of what has been done, only better. That is the programmatic approach, and it has been tried long enough. Any astute observer will notice that the mainline's ability to sustain its already-established ministries diminished long ago. For a time, some of these ministries may have to be given less attention until the local church base is renewed in its strength and has developed new sources of interest, leadership, and resources. This will be a hard pill for church bodies to swallow. A change of focus will require that spirituality, not politics, be the leading energy emerging from the mainline denominational centers.

Normative Behavior
2. *Make new-church development normative, not a temporary programmatic fix.* It is tempting to adopt new-church development as one more temporary emphasis meant to inject a bit of life into the mainline. Evangelism for four years; outreach to youth for four years; overseas mission for four years; justice and poverty for four years. New-church development must not be relegated to its own spotlighted moment in time and added to the seemingly endless panoply of causes promoted by denominations. The future of the mainline depends

upon incorporating new-church development into its matrix. New-church development is not one among many good programs of ministry. It is a thread that must run the full length of the bolt of cloth we call the church. The mainline must learn to move beyond the debate over whether new-church development is important ("Why do we need new churches when we have so many already?"). New-church development must become normative behavior within the grand scheme of mainline ministry, and the question of how many new churches have been started by Presbyterians, Lutherans, United Methodists, and the like, will become a benchmark for qualifying the strength of the mainline in the future.

Keep Denomination Young

3. *Begin new churches at rates that ensure that within 30 years, at least 30 percent of a denomination's churches will be under 30 years old.* Writing in 1991, veteran church consultant Lyle E. Schaller stated that in 1906, of 212,230 U.S. religious bodies, at least one-half were less than 30 years old. In contrast, in 1990, of 37,500 United Methodist congregations, at least 30,000 were more than 50 years old.[16] To counteract this trend leading to fewer and fewer young churches in aging denominations, Schaller recommended that every denomination or regional judicatory body begin new churches at an annual rate equivalent to 1 percent of the number of churches in its makeup at the time.

For more substantial growth, Schaller suggested a goal of 2 or 3 percent a year.[17] Thus, using the 1 percent goal, a denomination having 30,000 churches would aim to begin 300 new churches each year; at 3 percent, the number would be 900 new churches each year. The annual addition of numbers of new churches each year, combined with the loss of churches reaching the end of their effective years of ministry, will fundamentally change the capacity of mainline denominations to accomplish their *first cause*. Consequently, a renewed capacity to carry out important cooperative ventures in ministry will be realized as local churches again become the primary and essential sources of leadership and resources for these activities.

Pick Leaders Who Are 'On Board'

4. *Select executive leaders who are committed to the priority of new-church development.* Max DePree, writing in *Leadership Is an Art*, says,

"The measure of leadership is not the quality of the head, but the tone of the body. The signs of outstanding leadership appear primarily among the followers. Are the followers reaching their potential? Are they learning? Serving? Do they achieve the required results? Do they change with grace?"[18]

The task of systemically changing hardened denominational structures and practices will require extraordinary leadership. Almost certainly, it will require a different kind of leadership from what the mainline has had during its years of prominence, prestige, influence, and authority in American culture. Likewise, it will require leaders who are not bound by the task of *saving* the church and restoring it to its former ways. This enormously challenging task requires leaders who believe that the future of the church is more important than its past; who are willing to honor past successes, while letting go of old paradigms that no longer serve the *first cause* for which the church exists. It requires leaders who understand how new life can come to old denominations through new churches, and who direct their denomination's agencies and leaders to make new-church development a normative part of the denomination's purpose.

Leadership starts and stops at the top of any organization. Therefore, the first leaders who must champion new-church development as a fundamental goal of the mainline are the bishops, presidents, and other top executives of the various denominations belonging to this ripened family of churches. In the meantime, it will be difficult to find this kind of commitment and leadership in national and regional judicatory staff, in local church pastors, and in essential lay leaders.

Structure Follows Purpose
5. *Structure judicatory agencies to match the needs of advancing new-church development.* Today there is simply too much good-cause competition for a limited pool of mainline resources to make enough available to support a fundamental and systemic change toward a primary goal of new-church development. As demand for resources has outstripped their availability, the agencies, their assigned staff, and their advocates have become increasingly defensive and protective of their turf whenever any suggestion is made to reassign or reduce resources, staffing, or programming. Unfortunately, if a massive

and permanent effort to begin new churches is to succeed, the available resources will have to be used, in large part, for this cause. Presumably, in time, as the church at large is strengthened because its local-church base is stronger, more and more resources will again be available for other important missions and purposes.

Most mainline denominations simply do not any longer have the ability to fund from their center all of the worthwhile ministries that could be done. Therefore, each denomination's strategy should ensure that its primary agencies, staff, and resources are made available to advance new-church development. Whereas today it is difficult, if not impossible, in most national judicatory venues to identify the office and the personnel whose task is dedicated to new-church development, this office or agency should in the future fill a prominent and visible role among the denomination's various agencies.

Name Staff with New-Church Background
6. *Fill judicatory staff positions with people who are committed to new-church development and who have experience in new-church development.* No single leader at the executive denominational level will adequately lead a strategy of the scope I am recommending. This task will require a team of people whose gifts, knowledge, and experience are complementary and who together provide the utmost level of support for regional and local efforts to begin new churches.

Although I have met and worked side by side with many capable and committed denominational staff, too often I find that executives are selected and deployed to serve in these positions without much concern for what training or experience has prepared them to serve as the top staff member in a particular field. Being unprepared puts an untenable burden on the person asked to serve in this capacity, and the practice of naming staff without regard for new-church development has proved to be a poor strategy for furthering the advancement of certain ministries. A strategy that calls for a massive effort to plant new churches and to bring about a systemic change to aging mainline denominations demands staffing by unexcelled leaders. These people must be not merely academically trained in the field; they must have firsthand experience as proven leaders in local-church ministry. These must be strategic thinkers, as well as innovative ones. They should encourage improvisation and creativity as they work with fellow staff members, colleagues, or regional or local church leaders. They must have the attitude that their foremost task is to promote the creation of new churches, not the promotion of their own office, authority, or the denominational "line." They must be peers among peers, trusted and respected in the highest echelons of denominational leadership.

Put Money Where Priority Is

7. *Change the focus of spending, budgets, loans, and the like to promote new-church development.* In the North Carolina Conference, a great deal of money, mostly collected from apportioned giving (a proportionate "fair share") received from local churches' annual budgets, is expended for judicatory staffing, agency operation, disaster relief efforts, missionary deployment, bishop's compensation, communications, and other programs of ministry.

Except for some supplementary funding used to offset the cost of sponsoring annual congregational development training events and to lend money to churches for land purchase or building construction, nearly no funding is available from national agencies to give direct support to regional or local efforts to initiate new churches. Quite often, loans are more easily obtained, sometimes at lower rates, from local lenders than from the denomination's national loan office. I do not mean to be too harsh in my criticism here. These agencies and their staff, unfortunately, have little to work with and little to say about how their services can be improved. I think we have grossly underutilized the power of our denominational resources, and this habit has to change if the mainline is to move out of the doldrums into vitality again.

It is time for our denominations to ask some hard questions. For example, in our contemporary predicament, is it more important to fund missionaries who teach school or work in medical clinics—or to build new churches? Is it more important today to rush to every disaster site in the world with aid and assistance—or to build new churches? Is it more important to fund a national media public-relations campaign aimed at getting unchurched people to attend our aging, sometimes languishing churches—or to build new churches? I warned that these questions would be hard to answer. Our choices are not between good and bad, or between right and wrong courses of action. But we mainliners are losing our foundation, which has always been the local church and its ministries, and we will not stand long without a good foundation.

For many years, my family vacationed at one of North Carolina's beautiful beaches. Never choosing to pay the high rent for an ocean-front cottage, we always stayed at the same house on the third row back from the beach. But though we did not move an inch, our usual summer cottage became second row, then oceanfront, as year by year the relentless sea lapped against the houses in front of it, eroding their foundations until they fell in upon themselves and were washed out to sea. Whether we like it or not, something like this is happening to the mainline, so long as our aging churches continue to stand still, weakened in their ability to be the churches they need to be. For a while, at least, we must commit our financial resources to the task of building new foundations, so that some day other important, cooperatively supported ministries can again excel.

Perhaps the worst outcome of a national reprioritization of financial resources would be for national staff and agencies to so overregulate and micromanage the use of these funds that it would be difficult for regional and local agencies to be improvisational in their approach to creating indigenous models of new-church ministry suited to a certain locale. For example, the denominational funding agency might be overprescriptive in how the funding was to be used. Denominational agency guidelines might require that the money be used only for land purchase or building construction, even though the regional body's strategy called for the use of long-term leased facilities for new churches, and the greatest funding need was for compensating top-quality staff teams to lead in the formation of new churches. Preferably, a regional or local body that can clearly articulate and demonstrate its commitment to a strategy aimed at promoting the creation of vital and faithful new churches would be entrusted with using the provided funds appropriately and effectively. For example, upon demonstrating such readiness to create new churches, a regional body might request and receive a block grant for, say, $1 million. Having that million dollars, without restrictions or restraints on its use, might allow creative local leaders to negotiate another $2 million in low-interest loans or matching grants to accelerate the construction of efficient new facilities for new churches in low-income communities.

Seminary Training for Church Planting

8. *Require that denominational seminaries provide at least one year of intensive congregational leadership studies in their curricula.* When I board an airplane, I look into the cockpit to see if the pilot and co-pilot seem confident as they click on and off all the switches lining the panels in front of them. I suppose an airline pilot may have studied the history of aviation, and certainly I would expect that he or she has learned the essentials of aeronautics that explain what makes a much-heavier-than-air vehicle fly at 30,000 feet above the ground. But what I really want to know is: Do they know how to fly this plane?

Mostly, our seminaries do an excellent job of preparing clergy academically. Church history, theology, and biblical studies are their forte. I hold degrees from two of the nation's finest theological schools. The knowledge I gained there has been invaluable to my work as a minister, and my life has been enriched by the experience of being educated by some of the finest teachers in the church. But, for the most part, seminaries do a poor job of preparing clergy to lead congregations. Fortunately, most laity have figured out how to lead the church, with or without the benefit of experienced clergy, and they generously tolerate us during our trial-and-error period of learning by the seats of our pants (or skirts).

While studying for my master of divinity degree at Duke Divinity School, I served as a part-time student pastor at a small rural church. I was so green that I'm sure it showed in my skin tone. I was terrified by the task, so like any good ISTJ (a Meyers-Briggs personality type), I was determined to do anything and everything to overachieve and to prove that I was worthy of the call to be named pastor (or "preacher," as the minister was called in this community). One day, at the end of a meeting with the church treasurer, she looked me straight in the eye and said, "Preacher, people in the church have been talking about you." Every fear I've ever faced flushed into my face as I considered what trouble I had gotten myself into. But I had panicked needlessly, for she went on to say, "People are talking about you because you are visiting in our homes more than any preacher we've had for years. We didn't think Duke taught visiting anymore." I had to laugh as I responded, "Well, I haven't taken that course yet, and I don't even know that it's offered. I just didn't know what else to do with my time, and

I remember when preachers used to come around to visit my family, so I just figured I should do the same."

The need for congregational studies becomes particularly acute in the case of leaders deployed to begin new churches. If ever a pastor is on his or her own to create ministry, the fledgling start-up is the place. The possible roles of a new-church pastor are myriad: preacher, counselor, teacher, evangelist, musician, youth advisor, media and advertising specialist, land speculator, real estate agent, architect, construction manager, financier, administrator, computer specialist. Although these roles are important, a new-church leader will be prepared to create a new church when he or she knows how groups of people become a church; how a church's internal organizational structures are formed; and how lay and clergy leaders can work in concert to lead a church into effective ministry (and the list goes on).

One old preacher who was sent out as a young man to start a new church used to say, "They sent me out to start a church. They didn't give me any land. They didn't give me a building. They didn't give me a house to live in. They did give me a few hundred dollars to live on. So I just said to myself, 'I guess I better get with it.'" He gave birth to a strong congregation that thrives today. Having done it myself, with a little more to work with than that, I know how daunting the task can be and how valuable any knowledge about the nature of the church can be.

When the mainline begins its effort to begin large numbers of new congregations, the most essential ingredient to their success will not be financial resources, but leadership. Imagine if a denominational body begins, on average, 90, 100, 500 new churches every year. Who will lead these churches and how will these leaders be trained and prepared to lead them? If many of these new-church planters are seasoned pastors who are already leading congregations, who will fill their places when they move to new churches? Who will prepare these ministers to lead sometimes struggling, declining, and increasingly conflicted churches whose fears may overcome their capacity to carry out effective ministry in changing communities?

I suspect it will not be easy to persuade seminaries to tackle this task. I suspect that some judicatories will not want to prolong what has already become an increasingly protracted process of credentialing clergy. I suspect that some ministerial candidates will not want to add an extra year of seminary to their time of preparation without some assurance that the additional instruction will be rewarded. But if we fail to prepare a new generation of church leaders, especially for the creation of new churches, we will surely fail at the task of rekindling the mainline church.

Reward the Bold

9. *Reward regional judicatories whose leaders, strategies, and goals reveal courage, boldness, and innovation to lead the church through change.* If my memory from public-school science serves me, a boulder at rest perched on the edge of a precipice possesses potential energy. Push the boulder over the edge, and its energy is transformed from potential to kinetic. In the case of potential energy, the boulder's mass gives it the capacity to do work, although this capacity is not apparent. In the case of kinetic energy, the boulder's capacity to do work is realized when it is put into motion and consequently hits the ground below with great impact. I suspect that the mainline today possesses more potential than kinetic energy. That is, in some ways it is a sleeping giant whose internal functions operate well enough to keep it alive when it is asleep, but whose capacity for work is largely unrealized.

For the most part, constituent bodies' (regional and local judicatories, agencies, and congregations) conformity is rewarded by mainline hierarchies, whereas nonconformity—call it improvisation—is not so readily accepted. For example, one mainline denominational office has for years provided to all new churches, without cost, certain published materials. The package includes 25 denominational hymnals, a six-month supply of graded Sunday school material (also published by the denomination), a selection of baptismal and membership certificates, and a one-time discount on a purchase from the church's retail supply house. In monetary value, the package is worth several hundred dollars. On the surface, this offer seems generous. Donations of most kinds are helpful when offered to fledgling churches. Yet at least two other motives for this apparent generosity are evident. Clearly, the gift suggests that if the new church begins its worship and education ministries using denominational materials, it will continue to do so, creating a faithful customer for many years to come. One case of hymnals and a half-year's worth of Sunday school curricula will rarely suffice to supply the start-up of a new church, however. Second, the gift assumes that the new church will, of course, want to use *only* denominationally produced and approved materials in conducting its ministries, and that the Sunday school is the preferred means for providing Christian education and discipleship training.

Now what if it is discovered that worship in new churches is often best conducted using many nontraditional forms of music; that the preferred means for guiding congregational singing is to project music and lyrics onto large screens; and that Christian disciples are best trained not on Sunday mornings in a more-or-less public-school-shaped format, but through numerous small groups, short- and long-term, that meet at various times throughout the week and use myriad teaching styles? Would such new-church start-ups benefit more from the standard denominational donation, with the baggage of its assumptions, or from a grant that could be used to purchase the denominational materials the congregation finds useful? These might include a license to use copyrighted music from many sources; a projector and a screen for displaying songs, images, and video clips; or study materials from a variety of publishers to be used by participants in small groups for children, youth, and adults.

For many years my own denomination's national center had an office of architecture. The architect who staffed this office was helpful as a consultant to churches seeking his advice, but he was one architect in a denomination consisting of tens of thousands of churches. Because of its limited staff and budget, this office was not capable of providing design services to local churches, and no stock plans were devised for use by emerging new churches for first-unit buildings or for standard additions to existing churches. For each of their projects churches were expected to use local architects who would create custom designs for each situation. Less expensive design options and the use of stock plans from other sources were discouraged. For a church to receive a loan for building construction from the national loan office, the staff architect was required to review and approve the design plans. Obviously, these expectations and practices have encumbered many churches whose limited building budgets have had to bear the added cost of architectural fees (typically from 7 percent to 10 percent of construction cost). Countless hours have been spent unnecessarily by thousands of church building committee members whose task, in many cases, was to repeat what many building committees had done before them—to come to a similar end result distinguished from other building projects mostly by the color and texture of construction materials used.

What if a mainline office of architecture were to supply a plan book of basic designs for new-church first-unit buildings? Minor modifications in shape, or size, or types of materials used could be made from a palette of choices made available to a church building committee. A modest licensing fee, much more affordable than the cost of commissioning custom design work by an architect, could be paid to support the national or regional office of architecture.

So long as mainline denominational leadership maintains a frachiser/franchisee mindset toward its constituent bodies, conformity to implied norms will be encouraged and rewarded. This model may work well for business when a set formula for sales is found to be successful. It has been the staple for the success of many businesses like McDonald's. But the church is not a fast-food outlet. Its ministries must take on an indigenous form depending upon the needs it discovers in its own community. A congregation must have a certain freedom to improvise from time to time, ensuring that it can function as a unique body of God's people in its particular community. Top mainline leaders can discourage or encourage the local church to experiment with local models of doing ministry without asking it to veer from a commitment to its *first cause*.

Graceful Exits, Creative Closings

10. *Make closure of old churches a fundamental part of the strategy for new-church development.*[19] The challenge to start thousands of new churches in mainline denominations in the coming decades is matched by the challenge to care for dying old churches. Some of the causes for decline were discussed in chapter 1. More will be said in chapter 5 about what can be done with older, declining churches whose ministries have potential for revival. But in the mainline, we have thousands of churches whose predicaments have become so dire, whose community demographics have changed so dramatically, whose human and financial resources have become so limited in scope, and whose members' attitudes are so rigidly resistant to change that we must come to the judgment that the time has come for them to close.

Let me be quick to say that I am not unconcerned for the remaining members whose loyalty to a local church has been exemplary and whose faithfulness has enabled this house of worship to remain open for years beyond its capacity to function fully as a vital congregation. We must find ways to care for these people and to engage them in the greater church's ministries. Yet we cannot afford to have many of our clergy assigned to provide little more than hospice care for a clutch of members too small or too weak to provide vital ministry. We cannot afford to spend increasingly large amounts of our judicatory budgets to support and supplement the cost for staffing and operating these churches. If we are to begin numerous new churches, we will have to free up many clergy from their service to dying churches to provide the leadership to give birth to new churches, and we must liberate financial resources to accelerate the seeding of the church into new fields of hope through the creation of new churches.

Choosing the Right Remedy

A good friend who is not involved in church life, but claims faith nevertheless, has been told that his liver will fail him within three years. A liver transplant may extend his life, but he cannot be put on a waiting list for a new organ because he has no insurance. While he waits, bad habits such as smoking and drinking alcohol are out; rest and good nutrition are in. Taking these steps may help him feel better, and as a result he may live a few days longer than he would otherwise. But only the transplantation of a new liver into his body will give him a real chance to live to old age.

Rekindling the mainline church requires more than ending a few bad habits and taking up a few good ones. Revitalizing the mainline requires nothing short of its transformation into something demonstrably new. Programmatic remedies have been tried, and they have done little to attenuate mainline declines. It is time to try a systemic remedy. It is time to recall and claim that the planting of new churches in large numbers in aging mainline bodies has always brought renewed vitality to them.

Chapter Five

Do We Throw Away the Old Churches?

*The most innovative organizations do not change by
anticipating the future. They change by creating the
future.*
—C. Kirk Hadaway

How can anyone be born after having grown old?
—Nicodemus (John 3:4)

*The greatest challenge facing the church in any age is
the creation of a living, breathing, witnessing colony of
truth. . . . Can we so order our life in the colony that
the world might look at us and know that God is busy?*
—Stanley Hauerwas and William H. Willimon

IF THE INTRODUCTION OF HUNDREDS of new churches into the ranks
of old denominations presents a course of hope for these aging judicatories, what is to become of the increasingly timeworn and weakened older churches? Do they discontinue their ministries? Or is there
a way to re-create them? Will mainstreaming new churches into mainline denominations present viable models for renewal and sufficient
motivation to these older churches to cause them to be fundamentally reshaped into new churches themselves? Just as mainline denominations must engage in systemic change, so must mainline
congregations whose vision and mission have become dulled and

limited by the blunting effects of time find ways to retool themselves theologically and in practice.

A Dying Church Reborn

The rural Soapstone community for many years was the venue for a family-size congregation. Like so many rural community churches whose histories hearken back to the days when large families were the rule and when most such churches were sustained by younger family members replacing older family members, Soapstone Church, founded around 1837, served its community well for generations. Time and demographic movement took a toll on Soapstone Church. About five decades ago, its membership diminished to the point that its doors were closed and its active ministries were ended.

Though closed as a place of worship, the small frame church building and its nearby cemetery were maintained for a number of years. In time paired with another small church, Soapstone Church was reopened by leaders of its parent denomination. Students from a nearby seminary provided part-time leadership. A somewhat dilapidated mobile home served as a Sunday school annex. In addition to worship, its two or three dozen constituents provided a few ministry activities.

Suburban Growth

Time once again brought change to the Soapstone community. Suburban growth from a city whose center was more than 10 miles away reached and engulfed Soapstone's neighborhood. Despite the community's growth, few of the young and early middle-age, mostly middle-class, and affluent new residents who lived nearby visited or joined Soapstone Church. Under the leadership of its first full-time pastor, the Rev. Hope Morgan Ward, Soapstone's members began to question why the community was growing but the church was not. In short, the congregation's leaders discerned that Soapstone Church did not meet the needs of the new residents of the emerging new community around them, many of whom were well-educated professionals raising young children and youth. The church's facilities, including the small chapel and the converted mobile-home classroom, looked woefully sad and unkempt. Space limitations restricted the development of new ministry activities. The chapel size was too small to encourage the growth of a congregation large enough to give adequate leadership and financial support to a growing ministry. What little area was set aside for parking was unpaved. The church was situated on a road which, though once the main route through this community, had long since been bypassed by a wider and faster route leading into the city. The church was made no more appealing by a longtime next-door neighbor. He lived in an aging mobile home amid the new $200,000 to $400,000 homes, and defiantly flew a Confederate battle flag from a high pole in his yard.

A Bold Move

This little church could have chosen to maintain its quaint and limited mission for a season, perhaps in time diminishing in strength again to the point that closure was its only option. But instead, the congregation's leaders determined that the church needed to find a way to serve its new neighbors and that to do so would require relocation of the church to a new site and a new building, which would signal to the community's new residents that Soapstone Church was ready to grow with them, to invite them in, to serve them well, and to put them to work in mission and ministry. A seven-acre site at the corner of a major intersection a mile from the old church site was purchased. Grants were obtained from the church's area judicatory office, and loans were approved, allowing the church to construct a modest but contemporary church building.

For some of the old church's members, this step was not an easy one. I was asked to meet individually with as many people from the church as possible to inquire about their support for this radical disconnection from the historic location. Throughout one day, members and nonmembers who were active participants came by the church to be interviewed. Each scheduled session lasted about 30 minutes. Everyone affiliated with the church was invited to be interviewed. I began with a set series of questions, and everyone was given the opportunity to offer additional comments at the end of the session. Those who came knew that the primary focus of the interview questions would be relocation of the church. As comments were made and questions answered, I took notes and listened intently for some clue showing how ready these people were to respond to the bold and challenging task called for by the church's leaders. I heard a variety of opinions on the topic; most who spoke were at least warily supportive of the relocation idea.

A Critic's Support

Late in the day, an older man and woman—they were brother and sister—came in and sat down for their time with me. After they had responded to a few questions, the brother looked me squarely in the eye and said, "Mister, you see those gravestones out there in that cemetery?" He pointed with his finger out the dingy window of the trailer we were in, and I anticipated what he was going to say next. "Mister, my people are buried out there, and my family has belonged to this church for a very long time, and my sister and I, we don't like the idea of moving from this place one bit." I was not surprised at all by his statement. It was loaded with a palpable sense of nostalgia for the past, for the memories of family and friends, of baptisms and weddings and funerals and fellowship dinners and revivals and homecomings, and preachers who had been friends as well as spiritual guides. After what to me seemed a very long and quiet pause, he continued with what he had to say. This part I had not anticipated at all. He said, "Mister, we don't like this idea, but my sister and I have been talking about it, and we have decided that if the members of the church think it is the best thing to do, we will support it." I nearly slipped off the hard metal folding chair under me, so surprised was I by his deeply honest statement. I told him that I was taking notes on everything I heard people say, and that I would be reporting it back to a meeting of the congregation. I added that I had not been putting names with anyone's comments. But I asked his permission to tell the church that he was the one who made this important statement, and he graciously allowed me to do so. I suspected he might be a key influencer in this congregation, and I knew the impact his statement could have to help others see the value of change for the sake of the church's future.

Today, Soapstone Church, with more than 400 in worship each week, has a thriving children's and youth ministry; a high-quality child-care center; a large contingent of Boy Scouts; an active mission outreach ministry, including work teams whose members travel outside the United States each year; and a plethora of other valuable activities running seven days a week. With a largely white membership, Soapstone Church made a successful transition from its white female regenerating pastor, Hope Morgan Ward, to the leadership of an African American pastor, Leonard Fairley. The church is now engaged in its third building program since its move from the old site. To all but the few who made the move and who know the church's previous history, people who come to Soapstone today believe that it is a new church created just for their growing new community.

Another Story

Bethesda Church is a study in contrast to Soapstone's "born anew" experience. Formed in the 1960s to serve a homogeneous population in an emerging suburban community, Bethesda Church today is located in a richly diverse neighborhood situated on the border of Research Triangle Park, an internationally recognized high-tech research and business community started near the time when the church was begun. As the neighborhood has grown and become more diverse, the congregation has lost members and influence. Today, a few dozen members maintain a small number of ministry activities.

Aided by the church's area judicatory missions office, a new sanctuary was recently constructed at a considerably reduced cost to the congregation with the hope that the new building would cause the church to grow. To the contrary, congregational infighting has led to further decline in participation and the loss of financial stability. In 15 years, Bethesda has been led by six pastors. The church is now served part time by a retired pastor.

Each pastor has made good effort to lead Bethesda away from spiraling decline toward growth, mission, and effective ministry. Attempts made by the most recent full-time pastor to reach out to all of the church's neighbors, to integrate the membership racially and culturally, and to begin a new worship service featuring jazz music have been quashed. The advice of multiple congregational-development consultants, whose services have been compensated by judicatory offices and other grants, has mostly been ignored by leaders of the church. The future does not look good for Bethesda Church, whose nature, it seems, is to resist change.

Time to Be Born Anew

When Jesus invited Nicodemus to be born anew, he challenged Nicodemus to go against his nature to be re-created into someone new (John 3:1-7). The solution for what to do about declining older congregations is found in this notion of being born anew. Many older churches have to go against their nature, so to speak, to be re-created as new kinds of churches. Jesus' challenge may have been too demanding for Nicodemus. We are not told how Nicodemus responded. The challenge may be too great for many mainline churches. The powerful grip of a settled routine on a hardened, complacent system is hard to break. Attempts to break this grip often lead to conflict. Leaders who try to guide a church from its stuck position to a new manifestation of what it means to be church can be gravely mistreated by those who are determined to resist change at any cost, even if it leads to the death of their church.

The Paradox of Rebirth

Nicodemus was right to question how a person could go back into the mother's womb to be born again. It is a counterintuitive concept. But isn't this Jesus' point? Entering the kingdom of God is not a matter of becoming a better person or a more knowledgeable person or a more committed person, as Nicodemus might have supposed was the case. Jesus suggests that nothing less is required than going back to the place where life begins, becoming a creature not merely renewed, but made new.

Futurist Joel Barker describes how, when a paradigm shift occurs (A paradigm is a predictable pattern or way of doing things), everything goes back to zero.[1] By this, I think Barker means that no past idea, decision, or practice escapes scrutiny when a fundamentally new way of doing a thing is introduced. I believe Barker's notion of going back to zero is akin to the biblical idea of being born anew. When faced with a paradigm shift, assumptions about how the future will unfold become unreliable. Merely making old ways better does not ensure that a dysfunctional and ineffective system will be revitalized.

Saying No to the New

Barker notes that Swiss watchmakers, known the world over for their expertise in designing and constructing precision-geared timepieces, invented but ultimately rejected quartz watch technology. Though more accurate than most watches of older design, this technology did not fit the Swiss paradigm of what makes a watch a watch. Consequently, it was Japanese and then American entrepreneurs who saw the potential for quartz watches. Their capacity to rethink how to track time led their industries to surpass the Swiss quickly as the world leaders in watch sales.[2] For nearly a quarter-century, I have worn an extraordinarily reliable Seiko quartz watch that continues to keep time accurately—a testament to the company's success.

Think of some of the paradigm shifts under way—cell phones replacing land-line phones; e-mail eclipsing conventional mail; plasma-screen displays supplanting cathode-ray-tube computer monitors and TV screens; PDAs (personal digital assistants) substituting for paper calendars and notepads. I am heartened by the fact that people have so readily incorporated these new technologies into their daily lives.

When I consider that my father grew up in a rural community at a time before the availability of telephone service, and in a home once illuminated by carbide gas lights (considered at the time a significant advance over oil lamps and candlelight), I am amazed to see him punching away at the numbers on his cell phone. We can and do adapt to change, yet the church remains one of the most change-resistant associations in society today.

New Churches within Old Churches

I sometimes ask members of aging churches these questions:

- If we were here today, in the absence of your church or any other that now exists, would we decide to start a church?
- If we did decide a church was needed, what kind of church would it be?
- What would its mission be?
- What ministries would accomplish this mission?
- Who would be the primary recipients of this church's ministries?
- Who would be its members?
- What resources would be required to fulfill its mission?
- Where would this church be located?
- What kind of leaders would this new church need?

The answers to these questions are often quite different from the answers given to the question "What can we do to strengthen our church and make it grow again?" The questions I ask are the sorts of questions leaders of new churches ask themselves. Somehow, the future of many aging mainline churches will be discovered when older churches likewise ask what it means to "go back to zero," to be "born anew."

More and more I am certain that system-jarring congregational intervention is needed to carry some old congregations back to zero. Little evidence exists that other, kinder, gentler methods are working to bring about required changes. Simply, most people do not want to change from the way things are; when asked to change, they typically say, "No, thank you." So strategies aimed at inviting change or at tweaking an old, tired system seldom lead to the required transformation of a broken congregational system.

Entropy in the Church

In physics, *entropy* describes the incapacity for thermal energy to be converted into work. I see in many aging churches what might be called *congregational entropy*—by which I mean that a church's ability to convert its spiritual underpinnings into the work of being the church is degraded to the point that its members can no longer see beyond themselves to the greater mission. Congregational entropy is relentless unless checked. Soapstone Church, on the one hand, went back to zero by believing that its mission included acting like a new church for its growing, changing community. Bethesda Church remains resistant to being born anew and will continue to do so until its leaders decide that its mission is greater than care for its members and the perpetuation of their old pattern of what it means to be the church.

I earlier made the case that new churches somewhat naturally succeed at the formation of Christian community and meaningful ministry. And for this reason, I have tried to make a strong case for rekindling the mainline through an ongoing mission of new-church development. I propose that an effective strategy for transforming declining churches will be to begin, in effect, *new churches within old churches.*

My lawn is sown with fescue grass seed, which in my locale is reasonably resistant to drought, freezing, and heavy foot traffic. Once established, it is a tough ground cover. Fescue is an all-purpose variety of grass, one of several used in my vicinity for hay production and on highway shoulders, as well as for lawns. My neighbor has taken a very different course from mine, planting her lawn with centipede grass. Unlike fescue, which tends to radiate from its root system only a few inches, centipede grass is a galloping spreader that invades farther every year, replacing my fescue. If left unchecked, my fescue lawn will someday be replaced by centipede. In a similar way, I believe something like this can happen to resistant churches when a new strategy—"a new church started within an old church"—is followed.

Planting New Worship in Old Churches

Kirk Hadaway and David Roozen, in their book *Rerouting the Protestant Mainstream*, conclude that "the route to vitality is emergent in the increasing number of mainstream congregations that have their grounding in spiritually oriented worship contagious with the expectation, the presumption, the surety that God is present and active."[3] Spiritually oriented worship, they say, celebrates the experience of the presence of God; asserts the primacy of the experience of God; calls worshipers to a moral response to God's gift of all creation; and balances the urgency of action with the necessity of openness.[4] I concur with their conclusion that spiritually oriented worship is the most effective route to transformation of the mainline's aging churches. By planting many new (*spiritually oriented*) worship services in aging churches, the process of *starting a new church within an old church* can begin.

Accomplishing this goal may not be easy. I am not optimistic that many congregations, even those in serious decline, will readily choose to give up their current worship routines for others to which they are wholly unaccustomed. Sometimes, old worship will be allowed to stand alone until it dies for lack of attendance. But there is another way. Whether traditional or contemporary in form, new worship services can be started side by side with those already offered. They will in some cases be complementary to existing worship and in other cases competitive with it. In time, the worship services (revitalized old ones, or newer ones) proving to be most meaningful to a church's members and to its visitors will eclipse others in support. This is a parallel-development approach described by Arlin J. Rothauge, who calls it "walking together in different directions."[5]

New Styles Alongside Old

Parallel development might work this way: A small-town church, once a stable congregation whose ministries seemed adequate generation after generation, has been declining in size and activity for more than three decades. The form of worship has not changed. Year by year those attending worship are fewer and older. Visitors occasionally come and go, but few remain to become active members of the church. Decline is evident to the members, and concern for the future of the church is more and more palpable, but no one is anxious to adopt suggestions made from time to time by pastors and judicatory consultants. In her fifth year as leader of this church, the pastor invites a small group of church members to attend a weekend spiritual-life retreat. For some attending the retreat, the experience is a bit too intense and personal, and the worship led by the retreat leaders is not like anything they have experienced before. Simply, it is not an event they care to repeat. Others attending the retreat have a different experience. For them, the affair is transforming. They are moved by the worship services and by the personal expressions of faith shared by leaders and participants. They return home to their small-town church determined to be better church members, and they ask the pastor to help them create a new worship service reflecting many of the qualities of worship experienced during the retreat weekend.

So what is the pastor to do? Rothauge suggests that in parallel development "we neither put the two sides against each other in a win/lose battle, nor elevate one side to divine favor. In this strategy, we manage and maintain both sides concurrently. The leader supports both groups, or both sides of the situation, allowing both movements to continue their natural emergence and find their natural consequences."[6] The pastor, and perhaps other key congregational leaders, must walk the thin tightrope stretched between these two groups. The status quo group may feel threatened by the group wanting to begin new worship, thinking that this additional service may accelerate their decline. On the other hand, the venturesome group whose members have found the courage to try a new way of worship may feel constrained by the complaints of other church members who resist the idea of a new service.

Some level of conflict is inevitable. Conflict, at manageable levels, is not at all bad for a congregation since it can, in fact, act as a catalyst for change. Rothauge describes "bridge people" who work to create pathways of communication and understanding between people on both sides of the issue.[7] These people, along with the pastor, are instrumental to the success of the experiment of parallel development. In the end, says Rothauge, "we assume that one side will move to the background and the other toward the front—and the future. . . . It is even possible that some members of the congregation will pass over the bridge to the new dawning future that they had previously resisted."[8]

Worship as Key to Rebirth

For several reasons, worship is the most likely area of church life for change to take place on a scale sufficient to bring about systemic change to a congregation. It is the spiritual heart of congregational life; it is the single most cohesive congregational activity; it is most often the activity involving the largest number of participants; it is frequently the entry port for a newcomer seeking a place for herself in a spiritual community.

When carefully planned, a new worship service is begun in much the same way that a new church prepares for its first worship: Large numbers of people are invited to be present from the start; the invitation is repeated several times before the first service. The promotional effort is undergirded by the prayers of volunteers and church leaders who believe that God will be present in the hearts of people who are open to being engaged by a congregation that is ready to be the church.

Potentially, the first attendance at a new worship service offered by a declining church will exceed that of the existing service. The aging church's failing system can be overwhelmed by the flood of spiritual energy generated by significant numbers of people who have simultaneously joined together with the clear intention to become involved in worship and consequently in congregational life and leadership.

The Cost of Life Support

Too often, judicatory leaders have addressed congregational decline with the expectation that languishing congregations should be saved from closing at any cost. This has led some mainline denominations to have "welfare systems" pouring greater and greater amounts of denominational funding into supplementing pastoral salaries, facility maintenance, and programmatic expenses. In United Methodism this approach is manifested in many ways:

- An "equitable compensation fund" supplements pastors' salaries, ensuring that a guaranteed minimum salary is paid, even if the congregation served is unable to fund the cost and even if the number of people to be served are too few to occupy the pastor's time fully.
- A local church's goal to accept a proportionate share (relative to other conference churches) in its mission giving frequently is reduced, or the apportionment goes unpaid in part or altogether— with little, if any penalty (such as the future assignment to that congregation of a less experienced pastor) for its failure to contribute.
- Larger and larger numbers of small churches are combined by judicatory leaders with others in unrelated communities into multiple-church clusters to reach the critical financial mass required to fund a full-time pastor.

Welfare: A Sense of Entitlement

The longer these practices have continued and the more well-known the practices have become to the rank-and-file membership of our churches, the more an attitude of entitlement has arisen. Comments I often hear from some members and pastors of these churches include:

"They [denominational leaders] will never let us die."

"We've been paying into the apportionment fund for years. Now it's time for us to get back some of what we've given."

"If they would give us as much money as they give to a new church, we would grow too."

The worst thing mainline judicatories can do is to serve as welfare agencies for languishing churches. A better course, in my opinion, is for these denominational bodies to behave as venture capitalists. As an alternative to rewarding resistance to change, old-style thinking, and unimaginative leadership, denominational leaders can choose to reward with incentives those congregations whose members, leaders, and pastors choose to think as a mission people. These churches will be characterized by a willingness to change, an innovative and even improvisational attitude toward how ministries can be done, and a belief that it is more important to be the church (living out the *first cause*) than to be big and supposedly successful.

I once suggested to a large group of mainline executives that the funds used to supplement many pastors' salaries up to required minimum levels, in congregations too small to fund the cost themselves, should be used instead to give bonuses to pastors of churches whose members already provided at least the minimum required compensation, who chose to stay for extended periods in small-membership churches, and whose leadership was suited to serving the churches to which they had been assigned. In such cases, in my opinion, progressive, not regressive behavior should be rewarded. My proposal was received unenthusiastically. Most of the listeners' comments concerned what would happen to the weak churches whose survival depended upon long-standing supplements provided by the denomination. None were interested in having churches close on their watch.[9] No one was eager to face an anticipated cacophony of criticism from entitlement-minded, supplement-dependent churches.

A Pathway to Renewal

Where do we begin if we are to create new churches within old churches so that they may be born anew? In the following outline, I supply a framework for accomplishing this task. But each local congregation must find its own way to being born anew.

Triage for Churches?

1. *Identify churches willing to be born anew.* I first heard the word *triage* in news accounts of the Vietnam War. It seemed a strange concept at the time: members of a field medical team determine in a split second who is already dead or who is so mortally wounded that he has no chance of survival no matter now much care is given; who has

non-life-threatening injuries whose treatment can be deferred for a time; and who has injuries requiring immediate attention, which, if given, will likely ensure the soldier's survival.

I was again reminded of this term in the 1980s when Kennon Callahan, author of *Twelve Keys to an Effective Church*, worked with me as a resource consultant to assist 250 congregations located in my region. Though I do not recall his using the term *triage*, what he suggested was very much reminiscent of it. Callahan said that of our nearly 900 churches, about one-third were unlikely to need assistance in refocusing their mission; about one-third were unlikely to benefit from any assistance offered; and about one-third would benefit most from outside intervention, guidance, and support offered by my office and the team of consultant-leaders we had assembled.

To placate the concerns of some church leaders who thought that some of the most desperate churches should be helped and that some of the strongest churches (typically the biggest givers to the annual apportionment fund, which was financing this renewal venture) were entitled to some attention from our team, about half of the 250 churches we selected were from the weakest and strongest congregations of our conference, and about half were from the middle group that seemed poised to benefit most significantly from our help. A decade has passed since our "Vitalization Project" was concluded, and Callahan's counsel proved to be correct. Both anecdotal and measurable evidence demonstrates that the most significant benefits were realized by the churches in his "middle-third" category—churches that were most ready to make required changes leading to new vitality in their mission and ministry.[10]

The first step in a mainline strategy aimed at aiding older churches to find their new future as vital congregations requires a concerted triage process to identify those churches whose leaders are most ready to do what is necessary to create a new shape for the church's ministry. These churches should receive primary attention and resources from denominational leaders and agencies. These will be the vanguard churches, the examples that may lead others to follow new pathways in ministry.

A number of evaluation instruments are available to churches and may be used to identify the most receptive congregations to include in a renewal strategy. These include William M. Easum, *The Complete*

Ministry Audit (Nashville: Abingdon, 1996); Percept Group, *ReVision* program (Rancho Santa Margarita, Calif.: Percept Group, Inc., 1996); Kennon L. Callahan, *Twelve Keys to an Effective Church Planning Workbook* (San Francisco: HarperSanFrancisco, 1990); Leadership Network, *Leading Congregational Change Workbook* (San Francisco: Jossey-Bass, 2000); and Christian A. Schwarz, *Implementation Guide to Natural Church Development* (Carol Stream, Ill.: ChurchSmart Resources, 1996).

Pastors for Leading Change

2. *Prepare leaders to guide churches into new life.* Just as I strongly believe that not every pastor is suited to begin a new church, I am equally sure that not every pastor is prepared to guide a declining church through essential change. It has been said that past performance is the best indicator of future success. Often this statement is true, but I would add that knowledge is as valuable as experience. Despite their training, too few mainline pastors understand how congregations work. For the most part, seminaries attended by mainline pastors provide little training in congregational studies.

Many pastors, encouraged to participate annually in continuing education events, select courses and workshops, including graduate professional doctoral programs, that tend to focus on homiletics, ethics, theology, or biblical studies—but not so much on leadership development, congregational systems theory, conflict management, or congregational renewal. Renewal-ready churches will benefit from the leadership of pastors (and laity) who are keenly sensitive to the myriad dynamics at work in a long-established congregation.

A mainline strategy for church renewal should include training for its leaders in congregational studies. Much of this training can be provided by denominational offices or agencies, if the teaching staff is selected for acumen about what makes congregations thrive; for capacity to teach the leaders in training; and for past performance in effective leadership of congregational change. Interdenominational schools can be cooperatively developed (my first training in new-church leadership was provided by a multidenominational program known as JSAC, an acronym for Joint Strategy and Action Committee, to provide economic resources and to cross-fertilize ideas among participants from various mainline communities. Denominational leaders can encourage local church leaders to participate in work-shops and training regimens offered by parachurch organizations and secular leadership and business-development organizations.

To aid pastors in discerning their suitability to lead new churches, the use of tools like the *Myers-Briggs Type Indicator* (Consulting Psychologists Press, Inc.), the *Personal DISCernment Inventory* (Team Resources, Inc.), and *The Riso-Hudson Enneagram Type Indicator* (Enneagram Institute) is recommended. Used judiciously, with appropriate interpretation and application, these tools can be invaluable both to the individual using them and to judicatory leaders searching for people who can lead churches through change.

New "Stealth" Life in Old Churches

3. *Begin new churches within old churches.* A mainline strategy for renewing aging churches requires creating new churches from these old churches. As I have earlier indicated, I believe that the single most effective way to bring about this vitality is through the creation of new services of worship. In fact, I suspect that the greatest goal of a renewing church must be to recreate itself into a center of worship.

For example, I can imagine a church whose members and leaders determine that the annual budget and the allocation of space and staff time should all be directed primarily toward the creation of multiple worship services aimed at creating spiritual communities made up of longtime members and newcomers alike. Such a church might dedicate all of Sunday morning to worship, to the exclusion of Sunday school (which is more and more being supplanted by small-group discipleship and learning activities that may occur at times other than Sunday morning).

Additional worship services may be offered on Sunday afternoon or evening, while others can be offered on Saturdays and weekdays. A church following such a schedule says to its members and to faith-seekers in its community that worship is a primary activity of Christian community, that it can take many forms, and that it can take place at many times during the week. From people involved in a church's growing worship ministry will come the leadership for other vital missions and ministries. I am certain that phenomenal change will occur in many of these churches, and the path to mainline renewal will be incomparably advanced.[11]

Acknowledging Renewal Efforts
4. *Reward Innovation.* Reward and recognition are powerful motivators. Churches whose leaders take risks to create vital congregations can be acclaimed for their witness and for stepping out of old paradigms into new ways of being the church. A letter, a phone call, or a visit from a prominent judicatory leader extolling the efforts made by a church for the sake of renewal will go far to raise a congregation's self-esteem and to encourage its leaders to continue on their challenging course. Recognition of a renewing church's work before a large audience of denominational leaders, clergy, and representative lay members—such as at a session of a synod, presbytery, or annual conference—might encourage the acknowledged church to push on with its efforts and embolden other congregations' leaders to guide their own churches toward renewal.

Financial reward, in the form of stipends or grants awarded to local churches, can serve both as a means of recognition for work done or innovative work proposed, and as a way to ensure that movement into new paths of mission and ministry is not thwarted for lack of resources.

Like venture capitalists, denominational agencies should be interested in identifying worthy candidate congregations into whose ministries financial and leadership resources will be poured in expectation of good results. Venture capitalists act with *due diligence* to ensure that there is a good chance for their investment to yield a good return. They are willing to take measured risks to chance the opportunity for a significant return on their investment. They give guidance and assistance to those whom they support with their resources. They provide enough capital, not only to get things started, but to see their partners through to success. And when it is realized, they share in the success with their partners in whom they have put their trust (and their money). Mainline denominations whose resources and leadership are used in this way will be on the move, from a posture of preservation toward a posture of transformation.

Church Bodies' Purchasing Power
5. *Leverage the economy of scale.* Despite measurable declines in size and status, most mainline denominations remain among the largest social (and religious) institutions in existence. Their size gives these

judicatory bodies tremendous leverage for purchasing, borrowing, and investing, and the capacity to provide services on a scale unachievable by smaller denominational groups and emerging religious movements.

When congregations in equilibrium or decline attempt to transform their ministries, some retooling and capitalization are likely to be required. New equipment, renovation of facilities, and training for leadership development may be required. Alone, a congregation may be overwhelmed by these challenges. Working as an agent for hundreds and thousands of congregations, a judicatory agency or a multidenominational agency can broker deals on computers, furnishings, state-of-the-art audiovisual equipment, architectural designs, training, and consultation, lowering or perhaps eliminating some of these costs to a congregation. By leveraging its purchasing power, a United Methodist general agency can provide software to local churches at a cost unmatched by any retail source. Such savings on software may already be available in other denominations, as well. But software is merely a minor example of the potential leveraging power available to the mainline.

Moreover, mainline agencies may be able to negotiate with major lenders for large lines of credit, from which local-church loans can be made, backed by the denomination's guarantee of payment. Since presumably these loans would be made to those churches identified by a denomination as most ready to move into new forms of ministry, the risk of defaulting on the loan would be minimal. Working together, two or more mainline denominations may choose to combine forces to create their own loan fund. Investments in the fund, which become the source for monies to be loaned, could come from individuals as well as local churches and other agencies. I am aware that most mainline denominations have such loan funds available already, yet these funds are often inadequate to meet the needs of churches. They are frequently bypassed by churches seeking loans because of the cumbersome processes required to gain access to funds from denominational loan agencies.

The creation of a Real Estate Investment Trust (REIT), or something comparable, for the purpose of funding church building construction or the purchase of new or existing church facilities is another leveraging strategy. A REIT is a company engaged in the purchase, development, management, and liquidation of real estate assets. REIT participants invest in a professionally managed portfolio of real estate assets, which generally consist of properties that generate rental income. An advantage of REITs is the ease of liquidation of assets into cash, in contrast to traditional private real-estate ownership. Certain tax benefits created by REIT investment appeal to some investors.[12] This approach differs fundamentally from the way congregations have historically perceived their relationship to their facilities. Whereas congregations have typically owned their buildings, or at least functioned as trustees or stewards of denominationally owned buildings, ownership offers little benefit to churches. As an alternative to ownership, a church could lease its facility from a REIT. The REIT could sell the property to another investor or group of investors who would in turn honor a congregation's lease. The church could continue in a long-term leasing relationship or could choose to relocate to a more suitable location upon completing the term of the lease. The congregation's subsequent location could again be a leased facility (perhaps developed by the REIT to meet church needs), or the congregation could decide to purchase or construct its own building.

Architectural design is another function lending itself to leveraging by mainline denominations. Some denominations do a better job than others, but considerable savings can be passed along to churches whose ongoing and emerging ministries require new facilities. Only recently, a denominational office of architecture was discontinued after the sole architect on its payroll retired. Although the man was an excellent church architect, his role was primarily confined to consultation and plan review, not to the design of church facilities. No standard plans were provided by the denominational office. Aside from aesthetic elements incorporated into an architectural design, most church buildings contain predictably similar spaces with equivalent functions. This sameness seems particularly true for first-unit buildings of new churches. This has not always been the case, and I have discovered that all new ideas already existed in some form in the past.

For example, I have in my possession an undated manual (I suspect that it was produced in the 1950s) titled *Planning the Small Church,* published by the Interdenominational Bureau of Architecture "with the aid of a group of church architects." The booklet, priced at one dollar, represents the fourth printing of a collection of plans and suggestions "designed for ministers, field superintendents, architects and all interested in the erection and improvement of smaller church buildings." The booklet's introduction tells us that the "plans and designs . . . were prepared and contributed by architects who have devoted many years to careful study and service for the churches. They have given freely of their expert talent and their valuable time to make this publication possible. Their interest in the Church exceeds their desire for income or credit."[13]

The best church architects in the nation can be engaged by mainline bodies to design a collection of innovative and functional church plans that can meet the needs of the majority of churches needing new facilities. These plans can be adopted by churches, perhaps with a licensing fee for their use, at a greatly reduced cost compared to the traditional expense incurred for design services. I am not suggesting that churches work without an architect who is engaged directly with their project. I spent part of my undergraduate years preparing to become an architect. My doctoral dissertation is titled *The Symbolic Function of Church Architecture,*[14] and I am biased in favor of the use of an architect in church building programs. Yet I do believe that too much energy, time, and money are often needlessly put into church building projects, usurping more important uses of these scarce and valuable resources, because of the assumption that every church facility has to be altogether custom-designed.

Overcoming Barriers

The contributions made by new churches should not lead us to conclude that old churches should be counted out as venues for vital and effective ministry. But it must be acknowledged that if they do not alter the ways they have customarily functioned, many of these churches will continue to decline, and increasingly large numbers of old mainline churches will die in coming decades. Left alone, some churches will find it difficult, if not impossible, to turn toward new goals and new futures as Christian communities. Fuzzy vision, scarce leadership, and insufficient resources will often prove to be insurmountable barriers to transformation, even when a congregation's leaders are ready to guide it into new mission and ministry. But with the concerted and coordinated aid of its parent mainline judicatories, there is hope that the congregation's efforts and resources can be multiplied many times over. For this assistance to come to fruition requires the top echelon of mainline leadership to exchange willingly a routine bureaucratic attitude for an outlook focused on congregational transformation and the creation of a new generation of faith. Such an outcome may certainly require the work of the Spirit to be realized. So be it.

Chapter Six

Who Will Lead
New Churches?

The first responsibility of a leader is to define reality.
The last is to say thank you. In between the two, the
leader must become a servant and a debtor. That sums
up the progress of an artful leader.

—Max DePree

Those who try to convince us to manage from values or
vision, rather than from traditional authority, usually
scare us.

—Margaret J. Wheatley

So God led the people by the roundabout way of the
wilderness . . .

—Exodus 13:18

It was six o'clock on Sunday morning when my phone rang. The caller was Camille Yorkey, the pastor of a new church located in Wilmington, North Carolina. Only the week before, the church had successfully launched its first worship service in an elementary school gymnasium with 400 people in attendance. Camille was a veteran new-church planter, having a few years earlier started a church in a coastal community where rapid growth was fueled by an influx of retirees drawn to the area by the ocean, golf, low property taxes, and moderate winter weather. My conversation with Camille went something like this:

"Hello, Steve. It's Camille. It's snowing in Wilmington. What should I do?" Snow is rare in Wilmington, and for a moment, I thought she was kidding. But I could hear the alarm in her voice.

"You know we had 400 in worship last week. You were there. And you know that predictably only half that number return on the second week," she said. "And you know that if we don't get people coming to worship consistently enough in the beginning to initiate friendships and for people to start feeling connected to the church, we may lose them. People in Wilmington don't often drive in snow, and I don't suppose that the city has snow plows, so I think I have to cancel worship. What should I do?"

As her friend and colleague in new-church development, I would have a ready solution to her dilemma, she probably thought. I would like to think that my experience and wisdom as a congregational developer and former new-church pastor led me to respond to her in the way that I did. But in retrospect, I think it was an almost unconscious retort shaped more by morning irritability (I was asleep when she called, and early morning is not my best time) than by good judgment. In truth, I knew Camille's leadership ability, acumen, and good judgment, and I knew she could find her own solution to this unanticipated challenge.

"Camille," I said, "You are the pastor in charge. What do *you* think you should do?"

She thought for a moment, and then said, "I have lots of phone numbers from people who came to worship last week. I suppose I could go to the office right now, call all of them that I can, and tell them that I look forward to seeing them again next week."

"That's an excellent idea, Camille," I said. I hung up the phone, and Camille went to work making phone calls. Today, Harbor United Methodist Church, and Seaside Church, the congregation she earlier started, are two of the leading churches in worship attendance and faithful ministry activity in the conference.

Leadership Is Key

Camille Yorkey exemplifies the best of the kind of leadership required to create a new church. If the mainline church is to be effective at starting large numbers of new churches, the most important ingredient in that success will be leadership. Church sociologist Jackson W. Carroll says that one quality that stands out in successful churches, particularly those he defines as "new-style churches," is leadership that is innovative and entrepreneurial.[1]

Max DePree, chairman of the board of directors of furniture manufacturer Herman Miller, Inc., says, "Leadership is much more an art, a belief, a condition of the heart than a set of things to do. The visible signs of artful leadership are expressed, ultimately, in its practice."[2]

Margaret J. Wheatley, president of the Berkana Institute, a group of leaders committed to bringing positive change to organizations, and former professor of management at Brigham Young University, suggests that a leader's task is to communicate guiding visions, strong values, and organizational beliefs, keeping these things ever-present and clear.[3]

Where will the mainline find leaders like these—and I am thinking particularly of clergy leaders—who possess the leadership qualities required to begin new churches? Can pastors who are accustomed to leading "maintenance" or declining congregations effectively lead new churches? Can visionary, entrepreneurial, innovative, communicative, artful leadership be taught, or are these inherent qualities possessed mostly by a rare subset of leaders? Perhaps a conversation with church-planter Yorkey will help answer these questions. A proven leader, she has excelled at starting two new churches, has laid the groundwork for the establishment of a third, and has indicated that she would start another if given the opportunity.[4]

Thinking Like a Church Planter

COMPTON: *Camille, If you were selecting people to lead new churches, what most important qualities would you look for in them?*

YORKEY: I drove my parents crazy as a child, because there were so many rules that didn't make sense to me. So all too often I chose not to follow them if my parents couldn't give me an explanation to my one-word question, "Why?" Their "Just because I said so" was *never* a good enough reason for me to do what I was told to do. When I was a student at Duke Divinity School, Dr. Tom Langford, former dean of the school, was my professor for a course in theology. At the beginning of the semester I had to write a personal theological journey paper. I said something in my paper like, "When I was a child, I didn't take some Bible stories as factual, nor many of the premises for belief put forth by the church. I guess you could say I was rebellious theologically." Dr. Langford wrote in big red letters on my paper, "YOU STILL ARE!"

So, here's how I see it. We can hold to the core truths of the New Testament of 2,000 years ago. We can accept truths of faith set forth in the Old Testament. But, with our increased knowledge of humanity and history and science, we can make the truths of the gospel relevant in *new* ways for the 21st century. For this to happen, a good church leader has to *think out of the box*. I think this is a vital quality of leadership.

Another point about leadership is this. I believe that when people who choose to join a new church are permitted to be innovative and creative and responsive to the gospel in new ways, then wisdom wells up in their hearts, and you can see it on their faces when they know they have the freedom to *do church* in a new way. It is the leader's role to let go of preconceived ideas about what is needed in the church so that the Spirit can go to work. This, in turn, empowers a church's members to follow freely an appropriate path toward the goal of being the church.

Leadership requires flexibility. I think true leadership requires a person who does not have a black-and-white view of the right and wrong ways to be the church. If we open our eyes and ears to God's revelation for this moment, God's spirit blows in creative ways. Flexibility is a hallmark of good leadership.

Giving Away Power

COMPTON: *You have been successful as a new-church planter. To what do you attribute your success?*

YORKEY: I must begin by quoting you, Steve, because you have always said, "The only reason Camille is successful in her churches is because she doesn't do anything—the people do it all." Now, partly I know you are teasing me, but partly you are exactly correct. I go into any new-church project recognizing that the wisdom, creativity, energy, and heart of the church will come from those who by divine providence find their way into the new congregation. No one person working alone can make a church successful. In an earlier career in business, I learned that the sign of a good leader is that at the end of a project the people involved say, "We did it ourselves." Well, not only do my congregations think that—and say it—they *know it!*

The process begins immediately as I share my vision for the new church with its first participants, so much so that an image of it is imprinted onto their brains and being and they are convinced it is their own idea. I talk about who we will be as a people of God and a community of faith until they actually get the picture and believe it. I have always known that if I believe someone will make a difference and treat them as if that will be the case . . . they will! There is tremendous potential and power to be realized when a leader has "belief" in other people.

From the very first moment of the first gathering of the design team, core group, or whatever you choose to call those first few people who say yes to your invitation to create a new church, I let them know that they are making history. I say, "Document this gathering; take pictures; write down what we say; start a scrapbook; you are creating something important here; God is speaking in this place in a new way, and you are the ears to hear it and the ones to make it happen." I say this mantra so much that people jokingly quote it back to me all of the time. Once they are convinced that they have a role to play in making the church happen, the Spirit is present and it is a mind-boggling experience. We brainstorm constantly and use our imaginations until ideas, suggestions, and volunteers to carry them out seem to be bouncing off the walls. I never know exactly what to expect or what will be envisioned. It is my job continually to lift up theologically sound, what-would-Jesus-do type guidance to ensure that the conversations remain focused. When people leave one of these gatherings, they know that they carry the message of the gospel within them and they cannot fail. This is my leadership style. You might say I give away a lot of power. But I'm a team player, and at the bottom of my heart I believe that there is more wisdom in many than in a few. I just sort of let the Spirit happen.

This leads me to the second thing that I believe has made my new churches successful. From the beginning, the people who join me know that I am an ordinary person. My ordination gives me authority over word, sacrament, and order, but other than that, we are ministers together in the church. That brings me back to your teasing me about how I don't do anything—that I am the *great delegator*. It can appear that this is the case, I suppose, because when the congregation is bonded into tight-knit, loving, small groups, people know that someone will always be there for them when they are sick or in need, and it doesn't have to be me. Some would prefer having another member make a visit, if one is necessary, instead of me. Often, members are relationally closer to each other than they are to me. I'm always with them if there is an accident, or a death, or a surgery, or a critical situation. But think about it—God doesn't flow through me any more than God flows through other ministering members of the church. I don't have to be, or need to be, the only hand-holder; they can hold each other's hands, and they love being the ministers they are as they do it. If I did everything, including things they are very capable of doing, it would deprive them of the joy of ministry. How very arrogant and selfish it would be of me to think that because I have a divinity school degree, and am ordained, that God somehow should let me have all of the joy of ministry. My unique part to play is word, sacrament, and order; and I take those responsibilities quite seriously. But when it comes to ministry, it is my job to equip the laity so they are prepared to do *all* of that.

Remember when you came to preach for me in Wilmington while I was out of the country for two weeks on my 50th birthday? The church had been meeting for only eight weeks. We had almost 200 coming to worship on a regular basis. You said that you walked into the school that morning, and all you had to do was stand behind the borrowed pulpit in the gym and preach. That is because I never did any of the room set-up, or greeting, or fellowship, or any of the preliminary tasks required to be ready for worship. I never *had* to do these things. From the beginning, the people knew it was their church, and it was up to them to be the church. First- or second-time visitors would get a call from me, asking them to come by the church office to pick up a box of bulletins to take to the school on Sunday. Sure, I could have carried them to my car, and then into the school, but why should I? That would have deprived a new visitor from knowing how much she was needed by this new church. Give newcomers three weeks, and they were folding bulletins on Sunday morning; four weeks, and I might have them serving as ushers or greeters; and by then they were usually committed to the church. I don't underestimate the power of feeling needed.

The next thing I would say about leadership is this: From the very first meeting of future church participants, I try to build a sense of community. As people prepare to leave this meeting, they are asking for phone numbers because they have already begun to make personal connections with others. Before the first public worship service ever takes place, a loving, caring community of faith-seekers is in place. Newcomers are quickly incorporated into small groups so that they feel involved and accepted without delay.

Great Expectations

COMPTON: *It seems that you expect a lot from people who come to your church. Is this true?*

YORKEY: When I create a new church, I expect each person who joins its membership to find a place to serve. I also believe that a member should have only have one primary role at a time. There are three reasons for this. First, by focusing on one job, he or she will become so engaged with it that all of the possibilities and new ways it can be done can be investigated. Second, having only one job gives opportunities for others to offer their service. Third, doing so keeps "do-it-all" people from becoming the personality of the church and thinking that they own certain positions or have more power than others in the church.

Partly, I think that I have been successful as a new-church planter because of my attitude about money. No one becomes a part of the new church without making a monetary pledge in front of the congregation. It doesn't matter how much a person makes—10 percent of millionaire is the same percent of income as 10 percent of welfare. However, I understand that 10 percent is a lot of money for the unchurched who have never given anything to a church before. So I suggest that they start with some percentage of their income (I don't get into the before-taxes/after-taxes debate) . . . their heart will dictate, and then increase it as their spirituality and involvement mature. I model tithing for them, and they know that I tithe. In fact, before there are people involved in the new church, my tithe may be the only income for the new church. The people know that I know how much they give. Not all pastors can have this information without prejudice. I make it clear that I see giving as an indication of spiritual healthiness. I believe most people give because they see God active in their midst; they give because they have helped create the church's ministries; they give because they know what they are receiving from this new Christian community; they give because, in so doing, they feel good about giving back to God a portion of what they have.

The School of Life Experience

COMPTON: *How did you acquire these leadership qualities? I mean, did you learn them in a classroom, through experience, or are they simply part of who you are?*

YORKEY: Yes, all of the above! I have had many lives from which I have drawn leadership experience. I've been a school teacher, an executive director of a mental-health organization, a motivational speaker, a performer, a direct-sales representative, a crisis chaplain, a counselor, a goat milker and cheese maker (really!), and of course, a pastor. However, there were no courses offered at my seminary to teach me these qualities. So some of my leadership qualities come from experience and some come naturally, I guess. I do think that part of my success is because of who I am, formed by both positive and difficult circumstances in my life.

Nature and Nurture

COMPTON: *Do you think that good leadership qualities can be taught?*

YORKEY: I would like to say yes. Mostly, I have been taught what is most useful to me by my churches' members. There is a wealth of leadership information within most congregations if we listen and allow members to share it. Then, I have been able to model and teach staff at my church, and even leadership qualities to the congregation members themselves. It is more of an attitude. I had one staff member go from a new church to divinity school, and on to be an ordained elder. She was able to carry most of her learned leadership qualities with her. However, in some of the mentoring I have done with church pastors, it seems as though they are getting it and really do appreciate the information about healthy church leadership; but then it doesn't seem to make much difference in their actual church services or numbers or money. So I am not sure of the answer to that question. But I am sure that we should try. As a denomination and as a conference, we must try to offer experiences and educational opportunities and maybe even apprenticeships to teach the necessary qualities to pastors to be good leaders.

From Challenge to Opportunity

COMPTON: *What is your approach to dealing with tough challenges?*

YORKEY: I love challenges, and I spend a lot of time trying to figure out solutions to tough challenges. Perhaps it is because I am easily bored. Often, I can't sleep at night because of some challenge that must be figured out. Staff members have told congregation members that they have found messages from me on their answering machines upon arriving at work that I had put on their phones in the middle of the night with new ideas for dealing with challenges. I love to brainstorm with people. It is exciting to put a group of people together in one room and then let them come up with all of the possible ways to handle a challenge. Of course if the challenge is about me, or if someone in the congregation is fussing about me (which they often do), I take it very personally. First, usually I cry and then try to see the lesson that I am to learn about me from the situation. I pay close attention to how the business people in the congregation deal with challenges in their specific ministry areas and try to learn from them. There is no need to reinvent the wheel. Whenever I can learn from other colleagues or conference staff or congregational members, by all means I try to do it. However, it is very important when facing challenges to look for creative, innovative solutions that will turn challenges into marvelous opportunities.

Limb-Walking

COMPTON: *In jazz, an individual player is sometimes expected to be a soloist, given the freedom to improvise on the tune being played. At other times, each player performs together with all of the other musicians in the ensemble, following the chart as it was written. Do you think there is a time when a new-church leader should play the role of improvisational soloist?*

YORKEY: I think the leader of a new church should *always* be an improvisational soloist! Why would we start new churches that look just like our old churches? People could go to old churches instead. But new-church pastors must be strong enough to go out on a limb theologically, spiritually, socially, and *do* church in new ways for new generations of people. However, it is important that these new-church pastors be people of faith themselves with core values of the Christian faith.

Compromise and Consensus

COMPTON: *Have you found ways to share leadership with others without fearing that your role will be eclipsed by their success?*

YORKEY: I am *never* fearful of my role as leader. When they look good, I look good. My serious belief is that I am there only to equip them. I try never to stand in their way. It truly is the congregation that does the work that makes the church successful. Sometimes I think they work so hard because they know I can't do it. I let them tease me and make fun of my mistakes. We laugh a lot together . . . sometimes we cry a lot together. I let them see my brokenness as a human being. I also let them know from the beginning how very shocked I was to go into the homes of my first parish after only one year of divinity school. I was shocked because I found out that there was not a single family that didn't have a skeleton in the closet. There wasn't a single family that didn't have secrets (and they told the preacher!), and pains, and sorrows. I discovered that I was not a pastor in spite of my brokenness, but because of it, and I wasn't alone. So I know when I look out into the congregation each Sunday that I am talking to a hurting community and we are alike sharing our strengths and working together on our challenges. I preach to me, and if any of them connect to what I am saying, then that is icing on the cake. So when I share my real self, there is not much to fear about others rising up as leaders. They are needed as leaders. Oh, I've lost a few battles. But usually I try not to let it get to win-lose. It is much better if we all win. Compromise and consensus are the most healthy solutions to challenges.

How to Spot a Leader

Someone once asked me if I can look at a group of Asian people and tell who is Japanese, who is Chinese, and who is Korean. I responded, "Only by watching them walk." My facetious answer to my friend's question reflects my belief that being Japanese or Chinese or Korean is much more about how people live (*walking* according to the culture that shapes them) than about how they look. For example, do they *think* Japanese or Chinese? Do they *dream* Chinese or Korean? Do they *act* Korean or Japanese?

I was shown just how difficult it is to trust what you think you see when I had lunch with a pastor in an eastern North Carolina town. As we sat down, an attractive young woman came to our table to serve us. Admittedly, she looked Asian to me. Her name tag disclosed that her name was Tran. I thought this sounded like a Vietnamese or Cambodian name, so my mind quickly constructed my own presumed version of her history. With several Army, Air Force, and Marine bases nearby, I guessed that she was an immigrant from a southeast Asian country, or the progeny of a GI relationship with an Asian partner. All that I assumed about her made me expect her to speak with a distinctively Asian accent, so I tuned my ear to that prospect. To my great surprise, she not only lacked any hint of an Asian accent, but she spoke *perfect* Deep South English. I mean, the first thing she said to us was something like, "Hey! How are y'all today?" Spontaneously, I asked her, "Where are you from?" With a huge smile, she said to me, "I'm from a little town in Georgia. On the phone, people who don't know me think I'm a sweet little Southern belle!"

The task of identifying the ideal new-church leader from the church's general ranks of pastoral leaders is challenging. If we believe, as I do, that organizing a new church requires some unique leadership skills not always required when leading more long-established churches, then how do we identify these leaders? What are the unique skills required for success at the task of new-church planting? Just as I failed because of my presuppositions to identify Tran's origins correctly, I have learned that we cannot always judge a person's leadership capacities by what we see on the surface. We have to go deeper to see how they "walk" when working with people, when devising solutions to difficult problems, and when leading an organization through change.

Of the many qualities of good leadership, I have listed several below. Camille Yorkey's comments above reflect the presence of many of these qualities. Although any church leader would benefit from these attributes, they are *essential* for new-church leadership.

The Wisdom to See

A successful new-church leader is keenly discerning. Discernment is a skill—some would call it a spiritual gift, and I have no argument with that view. It has to do with perception, insight, and good judgment. I would compare discernment to what is called wisdom. A person having this quality seems capable of seeing things that are not always seen by others.

A friend who was asked to begin a new church from the remnant members of two small churches and a growing new population in suburban Chattanooga, Tennessee, recounts that he discovered a 30-acre tract of land that seemed ideal for a new-church location. Daily, he would go to the site, walk some distance into it, envisioning the church that might be born there. His judgment was good, his vision was transferred to the new church's founding members, and today the pastor's field of dreams is the site of one of the area's strongest churches.

Balancing Tradition and Innovation

A successful new-church leader is an imaginative pioneer. When I think of an imaginative leader, I think of someone who is creative, ingenious, inventive, enterprising, and visionary. Not simply seeing that a glass is half-full or half-empty, an imaginative leader asks: How can I find more water so that the glass is full?

I am constantly surprised at the lack of imaginative leadership exercised by church pastors (and laity). I am not sure if this is the result of too many unimaginative leaders finding their way into positions of church leadership, or if it is because somehow we have taught our leaders that creativity in problem-solving is unacceptable. Maybe we have led church members too often to believe that once something has worked for the church, it is immutable, for fear of turning our "solid rock" into "sinking sand." But the expressions "We've never done it that way before" and "We don't do things like that here" should be banished from the language. Tell me that you do not think it is the right thing for the church to do, and suggest your own idea for what to do, but spare me and the church these meaningless excuses for inactivity.

I am not suggesting that the best new-church leader is someone who is always going off half-cocked with indefensible ideas. Imaginative leadership is about more than seeing how unusual your church can be. Having circus-animal acts or pyrotechnic displays in worship are not proofs of the presence of imaginative leadership. Imaginative leadership is not bound by tired ways from the past, but neither is it uncoupled from the church's proven heritage. According to scholar Jackson W. Carroll, "As congregations move into uncharted territory, they have to exercise their freedom to innovate and create new strategies of action, but they risk being unfaithful to their calling if they think they can cut themselves off from a reflective conversation with the past or ignore the church's traditions. . . . The idea of a totally fresh start, free from the past, is attractive but perilous."[5]

Making It Work
A successful new-church leader puts creative ideas into action. The gift of discernment often extends to the leader's ability to take a creative idea and turn it into a plan of action that is beneficial to the people or the organization. This quality seems to be more prevalent in some people than in others. I think I have known more people who can *envision* creative ideas than I have those rarer people who can turn good ideas into workable plans.

An architect may devise a uniquely creative structure whose purpose will never be realized, if an engineer cannot find a way to make it stand against the tug of gravity. In their own way, successful new-church leaders seem to know how to balance an architect-like creativity with an engineer's pragmatism.

Effectiveness Trumps Busyness
A successful new-church leader values results more than activity. When Alson Gray was the presiding elder for a circuit of churches in the first half of the 19th century, his primary role was to travel the circuit from church to church, preaching, conducting worship and the sacraments, occasional weddings and funerals, and presiding over quarterly conferences, at which the church's business was conducted. Local church folk would provide him meals and a place to stay. Once finished at that church, he would pack up and head on to the next church on the circuit. It was not an easy life. The travel was rough at times; the accommodations were rustic at best. But the requirements of a pastor in those days were rather simple and clearly defined.

The role of a 21st-century pastor is quite different from that of Alson Gray. Many parish pastors today may preach from one to five times a week. Many are responsible for ordering the worship, typing the bulletin, and selecting the hymns. Writing and printing the newsletter falls the lot of some, as well. Some teach Sunday school, lead one or more Bible studies each week, conduct new-member classes, confirmation classes, and special studies. Other expectations include spiritual counseling, marriage counseling, hospital visitation, home visitation of every member at least once a year, and visitation of homebound members and those in senior care facilities. It is often expected that the pastor is responsible for setting a budget and seeing that all required funds are raised. Many people believe it is the pastor's responsibility to find new members, lead them to Christ, and make disciples of them. Some pastors are expected to attend all meetings held in the church. Some are responsible for opening and closing the church building, and for setting the heat and turning the lights on and off. In medium and large churches, the pastor is responsible for supervising a staff, which may consist of one person or dozens of people. Judicatory executives in some denominations expect pastors to complete and submit a sheaf of reports on time each year and to ensure that all mission support funds are paid. Pastors' families sometimes expect the pastor to stay home four or five nights a week, and to take one or two full days off for family time. Pastors are expected to complete a regimen of continuing education each year, to attend denominational meetings, and to be active leaders in community organizations. And finally, the pastor is expected to be spiritually mature, morally perfect, always friendly, and perfectly groomed and dressed.

I know that this description of the role of a pastor today sounds exaggerated, but the truth is that some or all of these things are expected of pastors today. It is sometimes said that what every church wants is for Jesus to be its pastor, but I'm not sure that Jesus would apply for the position. Such a perfect pastor would need degrees and lifelong experience in theology, church administration, business administration, human-resource management, youth ministry, psychology, sociology, architecture, gerontology, plumbing, and locksmithing.

In the 21st century, the pastoral role has become more and more professionalized, complex, and busy. As pastors have taken on this mantle, laity have often relinquished their roles as leaders of the church.

Members' demanding expectations sometimes lead to the perception that a pastor is failing at the role of the church's leader. Under this pressure, some pastors ship out, or are shipped out, with the hope that someone else can do better. In reality, all that may happen is that the same impossibly busy pastoral schedule will be expected of the next pastor and the next pastor, with each one predictably failing to fulfill all of the expectations.

Successful new-church leaders seem to know that strong churches in the 21st century will be led more by laity than by pastors. Then pastors can become primary vision bearers, keeping the church clearly in touch with its primary task of bringing people to Christ and making disciples of them. Pastors can become more like spiritual leaders than administrative leaders. Their role can be simplified, but made no less important than in the past for the health and effectiveness of the church. Effectiveness, rather than busyness, can be their measure of success. They can spend more of their time in making laity into ministers than in being ministers themselves. They can be healthier, happier, and more willing to serve the church during good times and bad.

Seer of the Vision

A successful new-church leader articulates a compelling vision. Whether thinking of Moses' vision of a promised land flowing with milk and honey, John F. Kennedy's vision of landing the first humans on the moon, or Martin Luther King's vision of the end of segregation, we know the power that *vision* has to draw people toward the successful accomplishment of challenging goals. A visionless church is a directionless church. Wheatley says:

> If we have not bothered to create a field of vision that is coherent and sincere, people will encounter other fields, the ones we have created unintentionally or casually. It is important to remember that space is never empty. If we don't fill it with coherent messages, if we say one thing but do another, then we create dissonance in the very space of the organization. . . . We end up with what is common to many organizations, a jumble of behaviors and people going off in different directions, with no clear or identifiable pattern.[6]

Somehow, we seem to have created church leaders who are not willing to accept for themselves the vital vision-setting role that is so important for a church's success. My own early experience in leadership training for the church makes me think that being taught that a *good pastor* is a *good facilitator,* and the propensity some of us have toward *enabling* behavior are factors making some of us hesitant to articulate a clear vision for the churches we lead. I am not suggesting that this *large* vision be set by one person in isolation from the thoughts and ideas of others. In fact, I am sure that the best vision for a church is one that is richly informed by many sources. But, ultimately, the leader of a new church can give shape to the vision and can communicate it to the people called to follow it toward the creation of a community of faith. Successful new-church leaders seem particularly adept at vision-setting.

Risk-Taker, Edge-Walker

A successful new-church leader walks on the edge. Some years ago, I visited the Grand Canyon with my family. My oldest son and I were determined to ride on horseback down a trail into the canyon. To our great surprise, when we arrived at the corral in the early hours of the morning, we saw no horses, only mules. Riding a mule was not exactly the image I had of myself as a temporary cowboy. As a boy, I had watched working mules on my grandfather's tobacco farm. When they worked, they worked hard, but I also saw how stubborn and ornery they could be. I began to imagine what it might be like riding a balky old cuss of a mule on a trip of a lifetime and I started counting up in my head the dollars it was costing me to do so.

Perhaps my disappointment was apparent, because the real cowboy in charge explained why we should all be glad that we were riding mules and not horses into the Grand Canyon. He assured us that the safest and surest way down and back was on the back of a mule, but he warned us that the mule we rode would walk every step precariously close to the outside edge of the trail, even when the trail was wide and more than adequate for his girth. Every word the man said was true. The slow and plodding mules traveled in single file down and up the trail, with each footstep hanging on to the edge of the trail. When asked why mules walk the trail this way, the old cowboy said, "They like to know where the edge is, so they won't fall over it—so they walk right on it."

As I observe and study congregations (especially new churches) to understand why some seem to flourish as places of ministry and mission while others do not, I notice that those most vigorous and effective are the churches whose pastors cause church members to hug close to the edge between safety (comfort) and danger (risk). They neither hug to the wall, far from the edge of the trail, nor do they jump off the edge of the trail into oblivion. I see this *edge-walking* quality in churches whose pastors demonstrate measured risk-taking behaviors to the congregation's leaders. This is often seen in churches that willingly experiment with how, or how often, or when God is worshiped by its participants each week; in churches whose members reach out and invite neighbors in from their community whose language, race, income, education, or appearance differs from their own; in churches whose members freely relinquish some tired traditions to make room for new ways to be Christ's church; in churches whose long-term leaders ungrudgingly pass along their positions to newcomers whose interests in and commitment to the church are evident; in churches whose pastors voluntarily withstand criticism for taking well-founded theological and moral and ethical positions that are contrary to the popular preferences of the church's members; in churches whose members do not hoard money in endowments and certificates of deposit while many needs in the church and community go unmet.

"Take Thou Authority"
A successful new-church leader freely gives away authority. A successful leader distinguishes authority from power. Think of authority as the right to invoke obedience, whereas power is delegated authority. In the United Methodist tradition, the ordination service for clergy includes the words, "Take thou authority." This conferring of authority could be interpreted in such a way that leads to an "I'm the pastor in charge" attitude—it's "my way or the highway." In United Methodism bishops are given the ultimate authority to place ordained elders in any congregation in his or her area, without recourse. Yet I have never seen a bishop exercise this authority willy-nilly, without

the involvement of a team of district superintendents whose wisdom and input is considered vital to sound decision making. When I consider Camille Yorkey's role as a new-church leader, I see this ability to relinquish authority in order to empower the people she leads as one of her secrets to success. She is always very much in control of the vision for a new church, and when she has to be, she can be firm in exercising her role as the lead pastor. Yet she, more freely than anyone I have seen, shares her rightful authority with almost anyone else who is willing to lead the church. Together, she and the people who join her become an almost unstoppable team bent on doing the right thing to create a faithful Christian community.

Effective leadership of a new church requires a team approach. Both laity and clergy benefit by working together, sharing authority, and exercising power, to find solutions to increasingly complex challenges faced by the church. Cooperation, not competition, is a key to successful team leadership.

Pioneer wagon trains and railroad trains, though increasingly rare as means of personal transportation, continue to be modes of travel we understand. Though their purpose is much the same—moving people and goods from place to place—the way these two transport systems work is very different.

A railroad train is tugged by a strong locomotive engine. Every car is attached to the engine in series, so every car must follow exactly the path of the engine and the other cars ahead of it. The train goes only where it is led by fixed steel rails. The engineer's job is to keep the train and its trailing cars on the track at a speed that does not lead to derailment.

By contrast, a wagon train consists of several wagons, each one operated by its own driver. Each wagoner is attached to the wagon train—not by fixed connection to other wagons, but by the choice to join other travelers on a common journey. Every wagon driver can stay with the wagon train or leave at will. The benefits of staying include safety, companionship, and the collective wisdom of all those involved in the venture about how to make the journey successful.

The leader of a wagon train, known in pioneer times as the wagon master, has the task of selecting the best trail, finding water and supplies, ensuring cooperation among the wagoners and their passengers, encouraging the travelers in hard times, and lifting up the vision of what awaits them at the end of the trail. But mostly, the wagon train leader has to keep all of the individual wagons moving in the same direction.

Effective new-church leaders work more like wagon-train leaders than railroad engineers. A railroad requires that every car follow the same path as the leading engine. The progress of a wagon train requires entrusting each wagon driver with the power to choose to stay with the train or not. Those who join such leaders can become leaders themselves. The church is the better for it, and all of the church's leaders receive credit for the success. I think this is what Camille Yorkey knows when she says, "I am never fearful of my role as leader. When they look good, I look good."

Treasures in the Fog

A successful new-church leader knows that chaos can be a good thing. Chaos often gets a bad rap. A pejorative view of chaos leads us to think of it as confusing, disorderly, unpredictable, and messy. Like some persistent hand-washer, we often respond to chaos in an almost obsessive-compulsive way by trying to eradicate it whenever it appears. Wheatley notes that our training urges us to interfere, to stabilize, and to shore things up anytime we see a system in apparent chaos.[7] But she notes:

> If we can trust the workings of chaos, we will see that the dominant shape of our organizations can be maintained if we retain clarity about the purpose and direction of the organization. If we succeed in maintaining focus, rather than hands-on control, we also create the flexibility and responsiveness that every organization craves. What leaders are called upon to do in a chaotic world is to shape their organizations through concepts, not through elaborate rules or structures.[8]

Not every pastor is comfortable traveling through a chaotic world as an avant-garde (i.e., innovative, pioneering, unconventional) leader. New-church pastors often are at ease with this role. Nancy Ammerman, professor of the sociology of religion at Hartford Seminary, says that pastors in status quo congregations rarely introduce new ideas. Instead, what they do well is to maintain the pattern of church life parishioners have come to expect.[9] "If they perceive any need for change, they [are] unwilling or unable to undertake the difficult (and often conflictual) work of dislodging old routines."[10] By contrast, many successful new-church pastors willingly lead parishioners into uncharted territory, into programs never tried before, and into new mission projects not previously attempted. When chaos occurs, such a leader may stand back, allowing its effects to be experienced by the church, expecting that some good can come forth from these disturbances in the status quo. A leader who embraces chaos knows that not everyone will survive the journey, and accepts this as an acceptable cost for doing what needs to be done. The leader's task is not to make everyone happy, but to carry the church to places where it needs to go.

Michael Slaughter, lead pastor of Ginghamsburg United Methodist Church, near Dayton, Ohio, admits that many members have fallen away from his large church each time radically new ideas have been introduced. Yet, even with these losses, as the church's ministries and practices have become more innovative, more people have come to the church, and the church's impact on its community has increased. It is said that when jazz saxophonist Ornette Coleman first debuted in the late 1950s, audiences didn't know how to take his innovative, improvisational style of playing. But notwithstanding audiences' extreme reaction to his playing, his break from past styles of playing set in motion his career as "the most significant jazz innovator of the last 40 years of the twentieth century, and opened up a viable broad highway on which what would become known as 'free jazz' was to develop."[11] These are examples of what it can mean to embrace chaos as a creative opportunity to discover treasures in the fog of what appears to be a state of disarray.

An effective new-church leader understands that plunging a church into periods of chaos, like a jazz player plunging a band into periods of improvisation through the "break," is what gives a church a capacity for resilience and metamorphosis.

Entropy and Renewed Energy
A successful new-church leader knows that order may portend decline. Entrenched routine is an insidious foe of the church. Even a church whose history includes periods rich with innovation can fall quickly

into equilibrium's trap. Equilibrium, experienced as a stable, ordered time in the life of a church, may portend decline. Yet a successful new-church pastor understands that a church's ministries can be effectively invigorated in the thick of entropy (thinking of entropy as a loss of the congregation's creative energy). To this point, Wheatley discusses Nobel Laureate in Chemistry Ilya Progogine's coined term, "dissipative structures," when considering a seemingly contradictory fact that loss of focus and energy are, in fact, an opportunity to create new forms of order. Says Wheatley:

> Dissipation describes a loss, a process by which energy gradually ebbs away. Yet Prigogine discovered that such dissipative activity could play a constructive role in the creation of new structures. Dissipation didn't lead to the demise of a system. It was part of the process by which the system let go of its present form so it could reemerge in a form better suited to the demands of the present environment.[12]

Prigogine's observations suggest that disequalibrium is a necessary condition for a system's growth.[13] This concept requires counterintuitive thinking, and this valuable leadership quality, it seems, is a quality more readily apparent in successful new-church pastors than in pastors who do well at leading status quo ministries. If a church is to remain healthy, its leader must understand when it is time, in a manner of speaking, to drop the next pebble into a still pool of water so that its surface is once again agitated into dynamic movement. Even a small disturbance can provoke a system, even a complex one, to respond by reconfiguring itself at a higher level of complexity, one better able to deal with its new environment.[14]

Putting Members in the Loop
A successful new-church leader freely shares information. Wheatley says of leaders, "We need to imagine ourselves as broadcasters, tall radio beacons of information, pulsing out messages everywhere. We need all of us out there, stating, clarifying, discussing, modeling, filling all of space with the messages we care about."[15] Successful new-church leaders are not stingy with information. They seem to understand that the vision for the church must be known so well by the church's members that it is second nature to them; that knowledge about everything—how the church came to be, how decisions are made, what

are the church's core values and beliefs, what resources are available and how they are used, who are the church's leaders, and what is the church's relationship to people in its community, for example—are fundamental to the success of the church. Therefore, a primary task of a new-church pastor is to broadcast important information so that the church's members are always clear about their purpose.

A Stake in the Outcome

A successful new-church leader builds consensus. In their book *Getting to Yes: Negotiating Agreement Without Giving In,* Roger Fisher and William Ury write:

> Agreement becomes much easier if both parties feel ownership of the ideas. The whole process of negotiation becomes stronger as each side puts their imprimatur bit by bit on a developing solution. Each criticism of the terms and consequent change, each concession, is a personal mark that the negotiator leaves on a proposal. A proposal evolves that bears enough of the suggestions of both sides for each to feel it is theirs.[16]

I suspect that this is what Camille Yorkey means in saying, "I learned that the sign of a good leader is when, at the end of a project, the people involved say, 'We did it ourselves.'" Fisher and Ury call this "giving them a stake in the outcome by making sure they participate in the process."[17]

Successful new-church leaders appear to understand that putting aside an ego-driven need to be "in charge" of everything, by sharing decision-making with others in the congregation, and the limelight when success comes, is an effective way to make a church's vision come true. Wheatley, echoing my earlier references to the importance of improvisation to jazz, says, "Improvisation is the saving skill. As leaders, we play a crucial role in selecting the melody, setting the tempo, establishing the key, and inviting the players. But that is all we can do. The music comes from something we cannot direct, from a unified whole created among the players—a relational holism that transcends separateness."[18] I believe that one of the worst enemies of the church is a leader who is consumed by the desire to know everything that is going on, and by the personal need to be involved (in an influential way) in everything that is happening. Add to this the desire to withhold important information from church participants, and you have a complete formula for overcontrolling leadership. Wheatley says that the effect of this kind of leadership is more of what we already have. "If we believe that acting responsibly means exerting control by having our hands into everything," says Wheatley, "then we cannot hope for anything except what we already have—a treadmill of effort and life-destroying stress."[19]

I have observed church leaders whose *apparent* success is derived through coercion. They seem bound to get their way at any cost. They belittle anyone who does not agree with them. They undermine the efforts of others who offer up their own ideas about how the church can meet its goals. They threaten serious consequences to those who contradict the leader's wishes. As a means to achieve objective goals, such as increasing membership or raising money, and as a means to keep subordinates in check, coercion can be very effective. But such disregard for the opinions and participation of others does little to create a Christian community built on relationships, respect for others, common vision, and a spirit of love.

Outfitting New Leaders

The need for land, buildings, and money pales in comparison to the importance of leadership for the success of a new church. Poor leadership is the bane of the church. Without appropriate leadership, a new church will be stillborn, and an old church will suffer an untimely death. Where do we find leaders for new churches, and how do we prepare them to lead?

1. Observe Past Performance
It is often said that past performance predicts future success. Though it can be a good indicator for predicting success, depending only on this proof overlooks the possibility that fair or poor performance by a church leader may be less a lack of ability than a pastor's misplacement in a church whose members are too hardened and resistant to respond favorably to direction. Without placing too much weight on past performance as a criterion in qualifying a leader to start a new church, officials should always review such information and discuss it with the candidate contemplating such a role.

2. Consider Personality Type

Personality type is another factor that may indicate a candidate's suitability for new-church leadership. I do not believe any one personality type or temperament is the ideal type for church planting. Having certain traits may be advantageous, but I know that shortcomings in personality can be overcome by knowledge, experience, willpower, and personal commitment to a task.

In the Myers-Briggs[20] scheme of things, I am an ISTJ personality. I always test out as a very strong introvert (I). One might expect that a new-church leader should be an extrovert, since a primary requirement of leadership, especially in the early stages of new-church development, is to seek out, recruit, and incorporate unchurched people into the core group of a new congregation. I do not find any of these tasks easy to do. It's not that I regard people with disdain. What I discovered in six years as the leader of a new church was that I could do all these things effectively, but at the end of the day, my emotional energy was depleted. I learned that whereas extroverts are energized by such roles, introverts are exhausted by the same tasks. I found some remedies for this cost to my well-being (most notably, daylong retreats in silence in the woods of the Appalachian Mountains), and the "STJ" part of me gave me much to work with to lead a young Saint Francis Church forward in its evolution. The sensing, thinking, judging parts of my being help me make decisions quickly; I am well organized; I make decisions with the "thinking" part of the mind rather than leaning on the "feeling" part.

3. Provide Appropriate Training

Most seminaries attended by prospective mainline ministers today are insufficiently equipped to provide training in the art of new-church planting. In my opinion, it is unlikely that, in the short term, seminaries will become the *primary* source of new-church leadership training. Absent this source of training, the mainline can take at least three strategic steps toward supplying training to people who seem suited to new-church leadership.

- Mainline denominations, independently or collectively, can create top-flight training events, study materials, and interactive Web-based courses.

- Mainline denominations can prompt their related seminaries to provide faculty, research, curricula, and practical, in-the-field opportunities to benefit students whose ministry interests include new-church leadership. Although seminaries are not likely to be the primary source of leaders for new churches, they still have an important role to play.

- Mainline denominations can build cooperative partnerships with parachurch and business organizations whose offerings in leadership development qualify to meet the needs of budding new-church leaders.

4. Generate a Cauldron of Experience

Nothing makes good steel like a hot fire, and nothing makes good leaders like actual experience. The best place for a future new-church leader to gain experience in leading a new church is *in a new church*. In fact, I suspect that many future new-church leaders will be laity who find their call to ministry as members of new churches. New congregations can provide invaluable opportunities for people to learn how new churches work. New churches can adopt the attitude that training next-generation new-church leaders is an important piece of their mission. Pastors of new churches can become mentors to promising leaders. Mainline denominational agencies may wisely invest in this important source of training by providing stipends to supplement the cost of adding internship programs in effective and exemplary new churches.

5. Coach New-Church Leaders

An athlete may have extraordinary talent, but the talent may not be fully realized until the athlete is properly coached. Michael Jordan, a good but not outstanding player on his high school court in Wilmington, North Carolina, burst forth to greatness once coached by the University of North Carolina's legendary Dean Smith. New-church pastors, with the aid of coach-mentors, often prove to be successful and satisfied with their ministries. Good coaches make good players. A good coach:

- gives advice to a new-church leader, but never demands that it be followed;

- asks a new-church leader good questions, and waits for the leader to find a good answer;
- generously shares knowledge with a new-church leader;
- celebrates success with a new-church leader;
- encourages a new-church leader when good effort fails to produce success;
- helps a new-church leader plan;
- encourages a new-church leader to take measured risks; and
- prays for, and with, a new-church leader.

If the mainline is to succeed at starting large numbers of new churches, and if these churches are to become effective communities of faith, and if church planting is again to become a systemic rather than programmatic focus of the mainline denominations for outreach and propagation of the faith, then high-quality, motivated, innovative, inspiring, risk-taking, spiritual leadership is essential. The mainline faces no greater challenge. No amount of money, and no degree of planning or research, will make up for ill-equipped, ineffective new-church leadership.

Chapter Seven

Can You Play Jazz on a Pipe Organ?

The amount of eccentricity in a society has generally been proportional to the amount of genius, mental vigor, and moral courage which it contained.

—John Stuart Mill

FOR MORE THAN TWO YEARS, I have been in the process of removing a century-and-a-half-old Appalachian mountain log cabin from its original site to a new location five miles away. It has stood upright against strong winds, cold winters, and deep snows. Its walls have sheltered many generations of sturdy mountaineers, but time has worn hard on this aged dwelling. Its upper logs are sound and wear their age well, but water and the weight of the cabin's walls, floor, and roof have brought decay and instability to its foundation timbers. Log by log, I have taken down this cabin so I can move it to its new location. But the task of reconstruction cannot begin until I have hewn new logs to replace the weak logs of the cabin's foundation. It will not stand without a new foundation.

Crumbling Foundations

In many ways, the mainline stands as a strong and vital institution. Its churches and its organizations, and the people involved with them, continue to influence American and world culture. Many of its missions and ministries remain viable. But increasingly, the mainline's foundations are crumbling under their own weight. Like the Sardis church, observers from inside and out are saying of the mainline, "You have a name of being alive, but you are dead" (Rev. 3:1). Increasingly evident is the degradation of the mainline's capacity to bring the message of the gospel fully to bear on a culture facing not 18th-, 19th-, or 20th-century issues, but 21st-century issues. Lacking the flexibility required to adapt itself to rapid change, the mainline is becoming less effective as a promulgator of the gospel. The mainline, like my timeworn cabin, has the appearance of being a sound structure, but it must renew its foundation of strong, vital churches, if its decay and destruction are to be arrested. Achieving this goal will not be easy.

In fact, rekindling the spiritual fires that first quickened the mainline requires system-shaking transformation. A catalyst is required to accelerate this required conversion. I have proposed in the preceding chapters my belief that new churches can fulfill this catalytic role in mainline renewal. Status quo leaders' resistance to new ideas introduced by new churches will be appreciable. As catalysts for positive change, new churches can pitch the mainline into a state of chaos. Chaos, though it might seem contraindicated for church health, is necessary to the vitality of a system like the church. If chaos is embraced as a natural and necessary component of church life, an open congregational system can be perpetuated, freeing the church to adapt to transitions in its missional environment.

The Butterfly Effect

Meteorologist Edward Lorenz once came to the conclusion that in a dynamic, evolving system, the smallest action can have profound results. He illustrated this point by noting that something as small as the flap of a butterfly's wing in Tokyo can bring about the creation of—or the prevention of—a tornado in some distant part of the world. This phenomenon has come to be known as the butterfly effect. The work of Edward Lorenz began a new field of scientific study called chaos theory.[1]

If asked for their opinion, most people would say that they prefer order over chaos. We tend to fear uncertainty, so we choose routes that are familiar when journeying through life. Whenever we experience chaos, we tend to interfere with it, trying to control and stabilize old, reliable beliefs and practices. Like most individuals, the collective membership of the church prefers predictability over chaos, as well. It seems that the older the mainline becomes, the more it disdains the turmoil initiated by disruption of the status quo.

Bringing Order from Chaos

Paradoxically, though order is mostly preferred over chaos, it is, in fact, from chaos that order often arises. Genesis describes how from chaos, God created order, giving form to the universe as we know it (Gen. 1:1-5). As a dynamic system, God's church can find its shape in the disequilibrium of chaos. Scientists explain that chaos works this way—order arising from apparent disorder—because some intrinsic boundaries always intervene, beyond which chaos will never go. So in spite of the apparently random activity introduced by change to an organizational system like the church, the system maintains an appropriate, if shifting shape, as a result of its own built-in boundaries. This means that we need not fear the effect of chaos.

Chaos creates the conditions for the church to be an open system. The church can meander in many directions, experimenting with how to be the church, ranging far from predictable pathways. But its boundaries, perhaps recognized in the church's core visions, values, and beliefs, will not allow the church to lose itself to chaos. The trait of a system that forms these boundaries and gives shape to the system is called a "strange attractor."[2] It can be said that the church's "strange attractor" is God, as known through the Old Testament, the life and teachings of Jesus Christ, and the traditions of the historic church. So long as the church's boundaries remain intact, no amount of chaos threatens its existence.

A Stagnant Pool

The mainline today is somewhat like a still, undisturbed pool of water. Still water eventually becomes stagnant, and leaders and members who suppress the stirring work of chaos prevent the church's renewal. The church leaders' task is to communicate the visions, values, and beliefs of the church to its members, constantly and clearly, while at the same time allowing individuals (and particular congregations) the freedom to experiment. Thus, the persistent, chaos-generating introduction of improvisational new-church activity into the still pool of an aging mainline can bring vitality to it without violating the integrity of the church's true purpose.

What does this mean, practically? If the church's purpose is clear and is adhered to by its leaders and members, then no change in worship style, music, architectural design, leadership style, program of ministry, or process of outreach to the unchurched can threaten the integrity or existence of the church. Though disconcerting, chaos is not inherently bad, nor is it to be avoided. Chaos is not the end goal, but an important medium from which open systems can emanate. If chaos is constant, then order is temporary—morphing in shape from time to time in response to changes in the church's environment. Creativity is born from chaos, and a creative church is responsive to a changing world, whose people constantly need to be reminded that God is good.

The Gift of Chaos

Chaos permits a system to be dislodged from equilibrium or decline. A small disturbance introduced into a stable organizational system can have a profound effect. Uncertainty is inherent to healthy organizations. Without some chaotic stirring, an organization, like the collection of churches we call the mainline, loses its potency. In their book *A Simpler Way*, leaders of the Berkana Institute, Margaret J. Wheatley and Myron Kellner-Rogers, state: "When individuals fail to experiment or when the system refuses their offers of new ideas, then the system becomes moribund. Without constant, interior change, it sinks into the death grip of equilibrium. . . . The system becomes vulnerable; its destruction is self-imposed."[3]

Generally, new churches act as open systems, feeling free to experiment with new ways to be the church. When inserted into an aging mainline, they can sharply challenge the declining mainline to break out of old, ineffective patterns of behavior.

Chaos: Reservoir of Creative Power

Creativity should not be confused with cleverness, faddishness, quirkiness, or caprice. Rather, think of organizational creativity as an exercise of imaginative resourcefulness. Call this simply "thinking outside the box," if you like. Uncertainty produced by chaos presents creative leaders with the opportunity to choose from a panoply of solutions to every challenge. Unimaginative leaders, faced with similar challenges, often shrink from the opportunities afforded them, by retreating to past ways retrieved from their organization's historic playbook. Yet "Stability is found in freedom—not in conformity and compliance," note Wheatley and Kellner-Rogers. They contend, "We may have thought that our organization's survival was guaranteed by finding the right form and insisting that everyone fit into it. But the sameness is not stability. It is individual freedom that creates stable systems. It is differentness that enables us to thrive."[4]

I often hear the argument in older churches that "traditional" liturgy and music is the right way to do worship, and that one Sunday service with everyone worshiping together is better than multiple services. Many new churches (and a growing number of resilient older churches) operate with the contrasting assumption that more people will be reached, and that the overall satisfaction with worship will be greater if multiple services having a variety of form are offered. This seems to be one of the factors leading to the rapid growth of many new churches, while some nearby older churches continue to decline in strength. So, it is in differentness (diversity) that stability (vitality) is realized.

New-church leaders and their young churches' members are inclined, sometimes more often than their counterparts in older churches, toward the exercise of imaginative resourcefulness. Creativity is demonstrated when its exercise leads to an organization's increased effectiveness, which is measured by how much the choices its leaders make promote its visions, values, and beliefs.

Order Originates in Chaos
Chaos-born changes do not exceed the boundaries of a system's visions, values, and beliefs. Says Wheatley: "Fluctuations, randomness, and unpredictability at the local level, in the presence of guiding or self-referential principles, cohere over time into definite and predictable forms."[5] Wheatley and Kellner-Rogers also observe, "We can't resolve organizational incoherence with training programs about values, or with beautiful reports that explain the company's way, or by the charisma of any leader. We can resolve it only with coherence—fundamental integrity about who we are."[6]

The mainline need fear chaos only in the absence of a clear sense of its purpose. Perhaps one of the greatest challenges to the mainline today is to articulate its purpose clearly to its constituents. I do not mean to suggest that the mainline is some monolithic structure that discounts important distinctions between its component denominations. But it does seem clear, for example, that fundamentalist churches, despite their individual peculiarities, have a much clearer sense of purpose than is the case today for mainline churches. Internecine debates within some mainline denominations (liberalism versus evangelicalism, homosexuality, abortion, and so forth) make it difficult to find consensus about the church's purpose. Yet, it may be that out of this seemingly chaotic time of disputation that the mainline will once again find a way to state its essential purpose.

If its purpose is clear, and if it is echoed by its leaders, in its goals, and by its practices, the mainline can give freedom to its individual parts to experiment with various forms of ministry with assurance that their actions will ultimately reflect the system's organizational principles. New churches, when again present in significant numbers in the mainline, will seem to some to be too unconstrained by past practices to become legitimate heirs of the mainline. But if the purpose of the mainline church is focused, and if it is communicated clearly to the leaders of these new churches, and if these rising faith communities echo this purpose over and over in every decision and activity, regardless of the new forms of ministry activity they choose for themselves, then out of chaotic activity will emerge forms that are faithful to the timeless aims of Christ's church. According to Wheatley and Kellner-Rogers:

> In a world of emergence, new systems appear out of nowhere. But the forms they assume originate from dynamic processes set in motion by information, relationships, and identity. The structures that we work within, the behaviors we live out, the beliefs that we cherish can be traced back to what is occurring in these three domains. How we treat one another, how we work with information, how we develop our identity—these conditions generate all varieties of organization.[7]

Chaos Is Messy

Folk musician Doc Watson sings a song whose lyrics repetitively ask, "Ain't life tedious?" If by tedious it is meant that life is monotonous, unchanging, drab, and tiresome, experience suggests that this is rarely the case. An individual may choose to live out this sort of humdrum existence, but life itself offers more challenges and opportunities than any one lifetime can embrace. A closed organizational system may function with rote behavior, with conformity preferred to experimentation. Though reassuringly predictable, a closed system's practices do not easily adapt to changes in its working environment.

Chaos studies take into account that the environments in which organizations operate are anything but stable and predictable. In fact, our context is messy. An organization that is best suited to thrive in life's messy environment is an open system. Physicist Paul Davies states, "Typically, complex, open systems can have incredible sensitivity to external influences, and this makes their behavior unpredictable, bestowing upon them a type of freedom." But he goes on to say that, surprisingly, "open systems can display ordered and lawlike behavior in spite of being indeterministic and at the mercy of seemingly random outside perturbations."[8]

Our best hope as the mainline church lies in congregations, new and old, functioning as open, not closed systems—sensitive to external influences, expectantly unpredictable, and at the same time guided by foundational principles that define their purpose. New churches are more likely to begin in the form of open systems than old churches are to move from their more conservative and restrictive ways to this more challenging, more promising form of church.

Wheatley suggests that a self-organizing system can freely grow and evolve. A self-organizing system is one in which the participants mutually and freely dispose themselves to the support of a common purpose. Wheatley states: "In a self-organizing system, people do for themselves most of what in the past has been done to them. Self-organizing systems create their own structures, patterns of behavior, and processes for accomplishing. They design what is necessary to do the work. They agree on behaviors and relationships that make sense to them."[9]

Life continues to be messy for a self-organized system. So long as it continually reorganizes itself in response to ongoing changes in its environment, it is positioned to remain a vital system. It is when a church functions as a self-organizing system that it best accomplishes its mission. Its shape is a reflection of its intended work. Following architect Louis Sullivan's well-known dictum, "Form follows function."

Planting Seeds of Hope

When a new local church is created, it continues to thrive so long as it remains an open system, free to experiment and to shift direction in response to changes in its environment. A thriving mainline depends upon trusting all its member parts—its congregations, new and old—with this same kind of freedom. Perhaps it is too much to expect that aging mainline denominations can willingly allow new churches to try out new ways to be the church in today's environment. But does the mainline have any other choice if it is to survive as an effective source of the Christian gospel? Can the mainline fulfill its purpose while remaining rigidly bound to its once-useful old ways which today have lost much of their capacity—like salt which has lost its taste (Matt. 5:13)—to bring change to the world? Is it the role of the mainline to direct its constituent churches into templated conformity? Or is it the role of the mainline's congregations, by the shape of their ministries, to give form to the mainline?

By now, it should be evident that I believe that:

- The purpose of the church is best achieved in congregations, not in the mainline's hierarchical and bureaucratic agencies.
- The most effective congregations are those acting as open systems, exercising the freedom to adapt their ways of doing ministry to the environment in which they find themselves.
- New churches, operating as improvisational agents of the mainline, can demonstrate to all of our churches the adaptive nature of ministry, when a changing environment requires an ever-changing response.
- Large numbers of new churches introduced in an ongoing way as a natural part of mainline ministry will ensure the vitality and effectiveness of the mainline as a whole.
- It is more important for the mainline to be a reflection of its vital churches than it is for the mainline's churches to represent a template of the mainline's past ways.

A Rekindled Bearer of Good News

When in Matthew's Gospel, Jesus asks if tasteless salt can have its flavor restored, the question is rhetorical, and the presumed answer is no. Yet, with God, all things are possible (Matt. 5:13; 19:26). When

I ask in the chapter title, "Can you play jazz on a pipe organ?" this too is posed as a rhetorical question, and at least practically, the answer is no. The immobility of a pipe organ makes it an unlikely instrument to be included in a jazz ensemble. So, in a way, it is analogous to the cumbersome mainline church we know today. Yet jazz combos long ago adapted the organ to their use when they discovered the versatility of the relatively small, electronic Hammond B-3 organ when it is connected to a set of spinning Leslie speakers. This same kind of adaptability is the mainline's challenge.

In an ever-changing world environment, can the mainline again become a rekindled conveyer of the good news to a spiritually hungry world? With God's help, and visionary leadership, I believe the answer is clear-cut—that even a bedraggled mainline can be restored to its place of importance as a powerful agent of the gospel of Jesus Christ. New churches will be the first seeds of hope planted for the restoration of the mainline.

Notes

Preface

1. I first encountered the use of the words *church planting* and *church planter* in reference to the process of organizing new churches, and to the people who start them, in Lyle Schaller's 1991 book, *44 Questions for Church Planters* (Nashville: Abingdon, 1991). This terminology is commonplace today among people in developing new churches. It seems to be an allusion to biblical accounts of God's kingdom growing from good seed well planted.

Chapter 1

1. Alvin Toffler, *Future Shock* (New York: Random House, 1970), 16.

2. Shannon Jung, et al., *Rural Ministry: The Shape of the Renewal to Come* (Nashville: Abingdon, 1998), 39.

3. Stephen C. Compton and G. Steven Sallee, *Growing New Churches: A Manual for New Congregational Development* (Nashville: Discipleship Resources, 1992), 2.

4. Stephen C. Compton, *The History of Chestnut Ridge United Methodist Church: 1832–1982* (Efland, N.C.: Chestnut Ridge United Methodist Church, 1982), 9-10.

5. Bureau of the Census, *Demographics of the U.S.: Trends and Projections*, 412.

6. Toffler, *Future Shock,* 16.

7. Jung, et al., *Rural Ministry,* 69-70.

8. Stephen C. Compton, "Edgar Gardner Murphy and the Child Labor Movement," *Historical Magazine of the Protestant Episcopal Church* 52, no. 2 (June 1983): 185.

9. Elizabeth H. Davidson, *Child Labor Legislation in the Southern Textile States* (Chapel Hill: University of North Carolina Press, 1939), 8-9.

10. The Rev. Johnny Branch, in a conversation with the author, recounted his childhood recollections of growing up in the Clark Street community.

11. Donald L. Metz, *New Congregations: Security and Mission in Conflict* (Philadelphia: Westminster, 1967), 32-33.

12. Jackson W. Carroll, *Mainline to the Future: Congregations for the 21st Century* (Louisville: Westminster John Knox, 2000), 72.

13. For various interpretations of the congregational life cycle, see Martin F. Saarinen, *The Life Cycle of a Congregation* (Washington, D.C.: Alban Institute, 1986); Arlin J. Rothauge, *The Life Cycle in Congregations: A Process of Natural Creation and an Opportunity for New Creation*, no publisher listed, n.d.; Alice Mann, *Can Our Church Live?: Redeveloping Congregations in Decline* (Bethesda, Md.: Alban Institute, 1999).

14. C. Kirk Hadaway, "The Impact of New Church Development on Southern Baptist Growth," *Review of Religious Research* 31, no. 4 (June 1990): 372.

15. Ibid., 377-78.

16. Ibid., 371.

17. For a brief synopsis of Weber's views on *routinization of charisma*, see Donald E. Miller, *Reinventing American Protestantism: Christianity in the New Millennium* (Berkeley: University of California Press, 1997), 25-26.

18. James H. Christie, *The Methodist Protestant* (October 1832): 338.

19. *The Oxford Dictionary and Thesaurus* (New York: Oxford University Press, 1996), 482.

20. Metz, *New Congregations,* 15.

21. Ibid., 37.

22. Ibid., 91.

23. Ibid., 39.

24. Ibid., 57.

25. Ibid., 76.

26. Ibid., 49.

27. Ibid., 103.

28. Ibid., 111.

29. Ibid., 49.

30. Ibid., 96.

31. Mann, *Can Our Church Live?,* 22.

32. Mike Regele with Mark Schulz, *Death of the Church* (Grand Rapids: Zondervan, 1995), 19.

33. Carroll, *Mainline to the Future,* 14.

Chapter 2

1. *UMC Local Church Profile* (New York: Research Office, General Board of Global Ministries of the United Methodist Church, 2002), n.p.

2. Joseph W. Watson and C. Franklin Grill, *North Carolina Conference Historical Directory* (Raleigh: North Carolina Conference Commission on Archives and History, 1984), 92-93.

3. In these examples, membership represents all baptized and confirmed youth and adult members.

4. *UMC Local Church Profile*, n.p.

5. Ibid.

6. Ibid.

7. C. Kirk Hadaway, "The Impact of New Church Development on Southern Baptist Growth," *Review of Religious Research* 31, no. 4 (June 1990): 370.

8. Ibid., 376.

9. Ibid., 377.

10. Ibid.

11. Lyle E. Schaller, *44 Questions for Church Planters* (Nashville: Abingdon, 1991), 28.

12. Penny Long Marler and C. Kirk Hadaway, "New Church Development and Denominational Growth (1950–1988): Symptom or Cause?," in *Church and Denominational Growth: What Does (and Does Not) Cause Growth or Decline*, ed. David A. Roozen and C. Kirk Hadaway (Nashville: Abingdon, 1993), 49-50.

13. Ibid., 56.

14. Ibid., 59. To determine the number of new churches started per 1,000 churches in a denomination, the authors multiplied the number of new churches started in each year by 1,000 and then divided this number by the total number of churches in the denomination in the previous year. "Pearson's r" represents the correlation between the new church start rate and the percent of membership change. A correlation of +1 means that there is a perfect positive linear relationship between variables.

15. Ibid., 75.

16. Ibid., 76.

17. Ibid., 78.

18. Ibid., 62. The authors seem to say that a movementlike denomination is characterized by the capacity to adapt to changes in its environment and a willingness to start new churches in times of strength and weakness. These they call resilient denominations. A denomination lacking these characteristics may have to use: its bureaucratic prowess to put in place a plan for new-church development, which, though more or less natural to a resilient denomination, is a relatively unknown field of work to many mainline denominations today. In Chapter 5, I offer suggestions for implementing a denominational plan for new church development.

19. Hadaway, "The Impact of New Church Development," 377-78.

20. Marler and Hadaway, "New Church Development," 83.

21. Outreach Marketing, Vista, California, sells predesigned print materials widely used by new church starts and existing churches for outreach and promotion.

22. Marler and Hadaway, "New Church Development," 86.

23. Ibid.,79-80.

24. Schaller, *44 Questions,*18.

25. Stephen C. Compton and G. Steven Sallee, *Growing New Churches: A Manual for New Congregational Development* (Nashville: Discipleship Resources, 1992), 2.

26. Schaller, *44 Questions,* 21.

27. *2001 Journal of The North Carolina Conference of The United Methodist Church* (Raleigh: North Carolina Conference of The United Methodist Church, 2001).

28. For more about the homogeneous unit principle, see various works by Donald McGavran, including *How to Grow a Church: Conversations about Church Growth* (Ventura, Calif.: Regal Books, 1973).

29. See Peter L. Steinke, *How Your Church Family Works: Understanding Congregations as Emotional Systems* (Bethesda, Md.: Alban Institute, 1993).

30. In the 1980s, Munsey Memorial UMC considered relocating from the inner city to a suburban area where many of its members resided. A Christmas Eve fire in a low-income senior citizen's residential center located across the street from the church led to the church's use as a temporary morgue. This incident greatly influenced the church in its resolve to remain at its present location, where it continues to have a vital ministry today.

31. Geoffrey C. Ward, *Jazz: A History of America's Music* (New York: Alfred A. Knopf, 2000), xvii.

32. Jonny King, *What Jazz Is: An Insider's Guide to Understanding and Listening to Jazz* (New York: Walker & Company, 1997), 14-15.

33. Albert Murray, "Improvisation and the Creative Process," in *The Jazz Cadence of American Culture,* ed. Robert G. O'Meally (New York: Columbia University Press, 1998), 112.

34. King, *What Jazz Is,* 7.

35. Murray, "Improvisation and the Creative Process," 112.

36. Stanley Crouch, "Blues to Be Constitutional: A Long Look at the Wild Wherefores of Our Democratic Lives as Symbolized in the Making of Rhythm and Tune," in *The Jazz Cadence of American Culture,* ed. Robert G. O'Meally (New York: Columbia University Press, 1998), 161.

37. Bill Evans, "Improvisation in Jazz," in O'Meally, ed., *Jazz Cadence,* 269.

38. Gilbert R. Rendle, *Leading Change in the Congregation: Spiritual and Organizational Tools for Leaders* (Bethesda, Md.: Alban Institute, 1998), 21.

Chapter 3

1. Some judicatory leaders and agencies may draw upon denominational strengths to provide program resources and leadership for new church development. A top-down initiated and supplied process that allows a great degree of freedom for experimentation by new church leaders may create an effective approach for generating large numbers of new churches.

2. Stanley Hauerwas and William H. Willimon, *Resident Aliens: Life in the Christian Colony* (Nashville: Abingdon, 1989).

3. By use of the term "church growth movement," I refer particularly to the work of Donald McGavran and Win Arn, both of the Institute of Church Growth at Fuller Theological Seminary, Pasadena, California, whose work, spanning at least three decades, has focused on removing roadblocks and creating new pathways so that churches can experience increased membership growth. Much about their work, including their well-known "homogeneous unit principle," has been roundly criticized for being too focused on growth at the expense of substance.

4. Seeker-sensitive worship refers to a model introduced in recent years at Willow Creek Community Church (South Barrington, Illinois) and elsewhere. Worship leaders require little participation from worshipers; few, if any, religious symbols, furnishings, or trappings are used; it is assumed that "seeking" worshipers have little or no religious background or knowledge about the Bible, liturgy, or religious language. The aim of seeker-sensitive worship seems to be the elimination of discomfort caused by participants' presumed unfamiliarity with traditional church practices; a nonthreatening environment is thereby created, one in which unchurched people are introduced to involvement in a faith community. In time, matured seekers graduate to believer/member status.

5. Lawrence Johnson, from a publication produced by Reconciliation Multicultural Ministries and Reconciliation United Methodist Church, *The Courage to Love Campaign: A Campaign to Support Reconciliation and Healing*, 2001.

6. C. Eric Lincoln, from a sermon preached at Reconciliation United Methodist Church, Jan. 16, 2000. Used by permission.

7. Mark Lykins, "A Confrontation with Love," *Virginia Advocate* (Nov. 5, 1998), 3.

8. Ibid., 4.

9. Ibid., 5.

10. Ibid.

11. Loren B. Mead, *The Once and Future Church: Reinventing the Congregation for a New Mission Frontier* (Washington, D.C.: Alban Institute, 1991).

12. Albert Murray, "Improvisation and the Creative Process," in *The Jazz Cadence of American Culture,* ed. Robert G. O'Meally (New York: Columbia University Press, 1998), 112.

13. Alyn Shipton, "Free Jazz: Ornette Coleman and the 'New Thing,'" in *A New History of Jazz* (London: Continuum, 2001), 773.

14. Hauerwas and Willimon, *Resident Aliens,* 18.

15. Ibid., 18-19.

16. Ibid., 14.

17. Ibid., 87.

18. Joel Barker, *The Business of Paradigms* (Burnsville, Minn.: ChartHouse International Learning Corporation, 1990). Video.

19. Hauerwas and Willimon, *Resident Aliens,* 123.

Chapter 4

1. Helen Bond, "Michael Dell Takes on the World," *American Way* (Oct. 1, 2001), 86, 90.

2. Ibid., 88.

3. The word *anathema* is fittingly defined by *The Oxford Dictionary* as an ecclesiastical curse upon something or someone detested by the church.

4. Bond, "Michael Dell," 93.

5. Ibid., 89.

6. Stanley Hauerwas and William H. Willimon, *Resident Aliens: Life in the Christian Colony* (Nashville: Abingdon, 1989), 30.

7. Jackson W. Carroll, *Mainline to the Future: Congregations for the 21st Century* (Louisville: Westminster John Knox, 2000), xii.

8. Bill Easum, "Ancient Mission in the Contemporary World," *Circuit Rider* (July/Aug. 2002): 25.

9. Janna Tull Steed, "The Duke's Faith," from an interview with Janna Tull Steed recorded on *UMC.org/Profiles,* 2002.

10. Marshall W. Stearns, *The Story of Jazz* (New York: Oxford University Press, 1958), 12.

11. Richard B. Wilke, *And Are We Yet Alive?: The Future of The United Methodist Church* (Nashville: Abingdon, 1986), 9.

12. James W. Holsinger, Jr., and Evelyn Laycock, *Awaken the Giant: 28 Prescriptions for Reviving the United Methodist Church* (Nashville: Abingdon, 1989), 131-150.

13. The United Methodist Council of Bishops, *Vital Congregations—Faithful Disciples: Vision for the Church* (Nashville: Graded Press, 1990), 9-10.

14. *General Minutes of the Annual Conferences of the United Methodist Church* (Evanston, Ill.: General Council on Finance and Administration, 1987, 2000). During the same period, lay membership within the denomination's Central Conferences (mostly comprising members outside the United States) increased by 747,924 lay members, clergy membership rose by 585.

15. Total lay and clergy membership for the United Methodist Church in 1968 was recorded at 10,252,958. By the year 2000, that number had decreased to 8,377,888, for a loss of 1,875,070 members.

16. Lyle E. Schaller, *44 Questions for Church Planters* (Nashville: Abingdon, 1991), 16.

17. Ibid., 12.

18. Max DePree, *Leadership Is an Art* (New York: Dell, 1989), 12.

19. See Beth Ann Gaede, ed., *Ending with Hope: A Resource for Closing Congregations* (Bethesda, Md.: Alban Institute, 2002). *Ending with Hope* grows out of the understanding that the closing of a congregation need not be regarded as a failure but can offer an opportunity for redirecting resources for new ministry.

Chapter 5

1. Joel Arthur Barker, *The Business of Paradigms* (Burnsville, Minn.: ChartHouse International Learning Corporation, 1990). Video.

2. Ibid.

3. C. Kirk Hadaway and David A. Roozen, *Rerouting the Protestant Mainstream* (Nashville: Abingdon, 1995), 129.

4. Ibid.

5. Arlin J. Rothauge, *Parallel Development: A Pathway for Exploring Change and a New Future in Congregational Life*, vol. 3, Congregational Vitality Series (New York: Episcopal Church Center, 1983), 15.

6. Ibid., 13.

7. Ibid., 14.

8. Ibid.

9. For an approach that shows how closing a church can be a strategy for releasing resources (people, money, and in some cases property) for new mission and ministry, see Beth Ann Gaede, ed., *Ending with Hope: A Resource for Closing Congregations* (Bethesda, Md.: Alban Institute, 2002).

10. All churches in the North Carolina Conference of the United Methodist Church were asked to conduct an initial assessment of their

capacities for ministry, using Kennon Callahan's *Twelve Keys to An Effective Church Planning Workbook* (San Francisco: HarperSanFrancisco, 1990). These churches were then divided into three groups according to the number of characteristics ("keys") that were strong. This assessment was used to determine which churches to include in the project from the group of churches whose leaders asked to be involved in the assisted planning process.

11. A growing number of churches are demonstrating how new worship services, when aimed at engaging the congregation's inactive members and unchurched community residents in worship, can cause overall weekly worship attendance to rise as much as 100 percent within two years or less. Dispelling the belief held by some that only congregations in growing suburban communities can increase in attendance and membership, three rural or small-town churches located in eastern North Carolina—Bailey UMC, Nashville UMC, and Jonesboro UMC—experienced, by starting new worship services, 50 percent to 100 percent increases in overall worship attendance within two years.

12. For additional information, see *www.REITNet.com*

13. *Planning the Small Church* (New York: Interdenominational Bureau of Architecture, n.d.).

14. Stephen C. Compton, *The Symbolic Function of Church Architecture* (Decatur, Ga.: Emory University, unpublished dissertation, 1990).

Chapter 6

1. Jackson W. Carroll, *Mainline to the Future: Congregations for the 21st Century* (Louisville: Westminster John Knox, 2000), 82.

2. Max DePree, *Leadership Is an Art* (New York: Dell, 1989),148.

3. Margaret J. Wheatley, *Leadership and the New Science* (San Francisco: Berrett-Koehler Publishers, Inc., 1992),133.

4. After the tragic events of September 11, 2001, Camille Yorkey was called upon to be a chaplain at the World Trade Center site in New York City, counseling ironworkers, police officers, firefighters, and other workers and volunteers participating in the rescue and recovery operation. Her book *Voice in the Wilderness: A Pastor's Journal of Ground Zero* (Burke, Va.: Judgment Ring Books, 2002) chronicles her time spent in and around the site and offers a message of hope and healing for all people in the face of this tragedy, interspersed with her own reflections on life, death, healing, and loving. Yorkey is the founder of Hope in the Wilderness Ministry.

5. Carroll, *Mainline to the Future,* 68-69.

6. Wheatley, *Leadership,* 56.

7. Ibid., 133.

8. Ibid.

9. Nancy Tatom Ammerman, *Congregation & Community* (New Brunswick, N.J.: Rutgers University Press, 1999), 327.

10. Ibid.

11. Alyn Shipton, *A New History of Jazz* (London: Continuum, 2001), 773.

12. Wheatley, *Leadership*, 19.

13. Ibid., 20

14. Ibid., 19.

15. Ibid., 56.

16. Roger Fisher and William Ury, *Getting to Yes: Negotiating Agreement Without Giving In* (New York: Penguin, 1981), 28.

17. Ibid., 27.

18. Wheatley, *Leadership*, 44.

19. Ibid.,23.

20. *Myers-Briggs Type Inventory,* by Katharine C. Briggs and Isabel Briggs Myers, is the registered trademark of Consulting Psychologists Press, Inc., Palo Alto, Calif.

Chapter 7

1. For more on chaos theory, see Edward Lorenz, *The Essence of Chaos* (Seattle: University of Washington Press, 1993.

2. Drawing from the language of science, Margaret Wheatley uses the term "strange attractor" to describe how a predictable shape is given to a system whose existence is lodged in the unpredictable realm of chaos. I think of this as a virtual, shape-inducing field (not unlike a field of energy or magnetism) that draws out of chaos the form required for an organizational system to accomplish its purpose. As catalysts for positive change, new churches can pitch the mainline into a state of chaos.

3. Margaret J. Wheatley and Myron Kellner-Rogers, *A Simpler Way* (San Francisco: Berrett-Koehler Publishers, 1996), 33.

4. Ibid., 41.

5. Margaret J. Wheatley, *Leadership and the New Science: Learning about Organization from an Orderly Universe* (San Francisco: Berrett-Koehler, 1992),133.

6. Wheatley and Kellner-Rogers, *A Simpler Way*, 60.

7. Ibid., 87.

8. Paul Davies, *The Mind of God: The Scientific Basis for a Rational World* (New York: Touchstone, 1992), 182.

9. Wheatley and Kellner-Rogers, *A Simpler Way*, 38.